LIFE ALONG THE WAY SERIES

BY **JOURNEYWISE**

A 90-DAY DEVOTIONAL

JESUS AMONG US

WALKING WITH HIM IN HIS MINISTRY AND MIRACLES

WHITAKER
HOUSE

Note: This book is not intended to provide medical or psychological advice or to take the place of medical advice and treatment from your personal physician. Those who are having suicidal thoughts or who have been emotionally, physically, or sexually abused should seek help from a mental health professional or qualified counselor. Neither the publisher nor the author nor the author's ministry or business takes any responsibility for any possible consequences from any action taken by any person reading or following the information in this book. If readers are taking prescription medications, they should consult with their physicians and not take themselves off prescribed medicines without the proper supervision of a physician. Always consult your physician or other qualified health care professional before undertaking any change in your physical regimen, whether fasting, diet, medications, or exercise.

Scripture quotations marked (NIV) are taken from the *Holy Bible, New International Version*®, NIV®, © 1973, 1978, 1984, 2011 by Biblica, Inc.® Used by permission. All rights reserved worldwide. The "NIV" and "New International Version" are trademarks registered in the United States Patent and Trademark Office by Biblica, Inc.® Scripture quotations marked (NLT) are taken from the *Holy Bible, New Living Translation*, © 1996, 2004, 2015 by Tyndale House Foundation. Used by permission of Tyndale House Publishers, Inc., Carol Stream, Illinois 60188. All rights reserved. Scripture quotations marked (CEV) are taken from the Holy Bible, *Contemporary English Version*, © 1991, 1992, 1995 by the American Bible Society. Used by permission. Scripture quotations marked (MSG) are taken from *The Message: The Bible in Contemporary Language* by Eugene H. Peterson, © 1993, 1994, 1995, 1996, 2000, 2001, 2002, 2018. Used by permission of NavPress Publishing Group. All rights reserved. Represented by Tyndale House Publishers, Inc.

Emphasis in the Scripture quotations is in the original.

Jesus Among Us:
Walking with Him in His Ministry and Miracles

JourneyWise
PO Box 382662
Germantown, TN 38183
https://journeywise.network/

ISBN: 979-8-88769-084-1
eBook ISBN: 979-8-88769-085-8
Printed in the United States of America
© 2024 by The Moore-West Center for Disciple Formation

Whitaker House
1030 Hunt Valley Circle
New Kensington, PA 15068
www.whitakerhouse.com

Library of Congress Control Number: 2023948589

1 2 3 4 5 6 7 8 9 10 11 ⑾ 31 30 29 28 27 26 25 24

CONTENTS

FOREWORD

Therefore, as you received Christ Jesus the Lord, so walk in him, rooted and built up in him and established in the faith, just as you were taught, abounding in thanksgiving.

Colossians 2:6–7 ESV

In *Jesus with Us*—the first leg of the Life Along the Way Series—God came to earth in Jesus Christ to be with us, close to us, and in relationship with us. It's in His very name, as Matthew 1:23 tells us that *Immanuel* means "God with us."

In this second leg of the series, as we continue on a one-year journey with Jesus, we learn of the ministry and miracles that are possible when we have *Jesus Among Us.*

As we set out into this intimate devotional, we will explore several interactions Jesus had with people along the way, including those in need of miracles, those in search of deep inclusion into the family, and many simply craving the basic power of touch. Farther along the road, as we learn more about our travel companions and the One who calls us to follow, we also learn about ourselves.

In this part of your year-long exploration, the idea and importance of "knowing and being known" become a critical intersection for those experiencing the teachings, interactions, and love of Jesus, settling in and allowing our sense of awe to transform into practical lessons for each day.

In the first-century church, travel required substantial effort and planning. The time spent traveling afforded not only a *deeper* picture of the journey but a *bigger* picture as well, enabling people to come to a better understanding of purpose, development, and destination.

We have the privilege of traveling through life with the greatest Teacher, Friend, and Savior we could ever know. He invites you, at any point in your journey, to ask the questions that lie deep in your soul and spend time pondering how each answer fits within the context of the Great Answer of Jesus.

As with any trip, to arrive at your desired destination, you must remain faithful and consistent. Yes, each leg of the journey starts with the first step—but it continues with the next step and the next, putting one foot in front of the other and never giving up.

If you want to finish well, the next step you take—the next commitment, the next act of faithfulness—matters. Don't give up; give in to where the road leads.

Walking you through that spiritual development, this second devotional in the Life Along the Way Series invites you to encounter *Jesus Among Us* as you go to work, the holy places, common everyday spaces, and everywhere in between.

To walk with Jesus through His earthly life—as a friend and fellow traveler on the road—is to witness a holy God enter into humanity's journey and make it His own in order to redeem us and give us true life.

As we join Jesus on this part of the journey, we stop at important intersections of places, people, and circumstances that give us a deeper glimpse into God's heart for us by watching His Son walk among us.

Where are you in your journey with Jesus? To meet Him at the beginning is a divine discovery, but to set out on the road with Him as He teaches, heals, and guides us in His love is powerful, personal, and full of purpose that we can carry into every day.

As you read this devotional, I encourage you to reflect on the humanity of Jesus's earthly journey. Listen to His conversations with family members and friends. Hear the Father give Him His next directions and destinations. Watch the equally human and divine story of Jesus unfold before your eyes.

I pray that by doing so, you will find yourself walking ever more closely with the One who is always with us and among us.

—*Shane Stanford*
Founder and CEO, The Moore-West Center for Applied Theology
President, JourneyWise

WALKING WITH POWER AND PURPOSE

After Jesus's early ministry was established, Jesus continued to travel with His disciples and teach people all over the region through sermons and parables. Much to the astonishment and wonder of many of His onlookers, Jesus's teachings came with an unparalleled authority and power—not just in the nature of His words but also in the miracles that accompanied them.

These miracles showed that Jesus's authority came directly from God. They demonstrated His power over sickness and health, over the earth's elements, and even over death. Many viewers were drawn in by these acts of power but never let their significance fully sink in. They remained awed by the spectacle but failed to see the larger picture behind the works. Similarly, they often failed to listen to the words coming out of Jesus's mouth. Words that would guide them into new lives, ones filled with hope and meaning.

As we continue our journey in the Life Along the Way Series with book two, *Jesus Among Us: Walking with Him in His Ministry and Miracles*, it's essential that we keep our ears and eyes open. When we do, we can see that Jesus's miracles reveal His compassion and His power, and that His parabolic teachings further clarify both His calling on our lives and what our acceptance of His presence can bring to us. Walking through these powerful moments with Jesus and His disciples, we can rest assured that He does have the ability to heal and save, both physically and spiritually.

Jesus's first disciples experienced His authority and power as they walked with Him daily. Over time, this same power and sense of authority was dispersed to them, so they could continue sharing the good news and lead the lives God had waiting for them. The same can be true for us when we walk with Jesus daily through the Scriptures; because, honestly, we simply cannot travel with Jesus without experiencing His power along the way. As we watch our lives shift and change, and look back at everything He's done, His potent miracles become unforgettable markers along the path. And, through it all, we are drawn more deeply to our life's true purpose and the freedom that comes with living in God's love.

If you are new to this series, we created the four Life Along the Way daily devotionals to capture the essence of Jesus's life, ministry, death, and ascension. And you are holding in your hands book two. (While we encourage you to read the books sequentially, you may read them in any order you choose.)

Each devotional is designed to be read in ninety days, but you can just as easily go at your own pace. It's okay if you get behind or if you read ahead. It's okay if it takes you a year to go through each book. The idea is that you're getting to know the journey of Jesus and allowing His journey to shape and direct yours.

The four Life Along the Way books are as follows:

1. *Jesus with Us: Meeting Him Where He Began*

2. *Jesus Among Us: Walking with Him in His Ministry and Miracles*

3. *Jesus Through Us: Following His Example in Love and Service*

4. *Jesus in Us: Living Wholeheartedly the Life He Intends*

Whether you've been in the church your whole life, are a curious skeptic, or find yourself somewhere in between, we hope that this journey through Scripture focused on the way Jesus "did life" will add great purpose to your *Life Along the Way*. We trust that God will give you wisdom for the journey as He grows you into His likeness and that you will be transformed as you live daily with Jesus.

Second Corinthians 3:18 says, *"And we all, who with unveiled faces contemplate the Lord's glory, are being transformed into his image with ever-increasing glory, which comes from the Lord, who is the Spirit"* (NIV).

As you journey with Jesus, our hope is that you would *love Jesus and love like Jesus.*

Let's jump back on the road and get rolling!

—*The JourneyWise Team*

DAY 1:
OUR CHOSEN PATH

SCRIPTURE READING

MATTHEW 7:13–14 (NIV)

Enter through the narrow gate. For wide is the gate and broad is the road that leads to destruction, and many enter through it. But small is the gate and narrow the road that leads to life, and only a few find it.

LIFE LESSONS

Life is a series of choices—decisions that we make all the time, every day, both large and small. These threads of choices lead us down our life path, our journey. We will follow one of two distinct paths: One path will be easier because it won't require much in the way of hard changes. It'll let us keep doing exactly what we're already doing and what we like to do, whether it's good for us or not. This means we get to stay within our comfort zone—keeping to our usual lifestyles and habits and focusing on ourselves. The other path will mean going deep inside ourselves, listening to God, and shifting the focus of our hearts to align with His. It'll mean making some harder decisions that won't always be understood by those around us, decisions that go against today's culture.

The first path chooses the world—with its comforts, conveniences, and temporary good feelings. The second chooses Jesus, which involves our being truly transformed from the inside out by following Him and becoming like Him.

It can be tempting to do what's easiest and requires the least resistance. On that path, you don't have to work at anything new. You don't have to change. You can do what everyone else is doing. But the genuine Christian life is "the road less traveled." It is seen as the harder path because it requires giving up your own plans and making decisions with eternity—instead of just today—in mind. However, the hardship on this path is only momentary discomfort in the face of the wonderful things to come: an eternity with Jesus, being held in God's hands, and knowing that you are never alone. That journey is well worth it!

WHERE ARE YOU?

In what ways do you find yourself sticking to your comfort zone, even though it may not be the best place for you?

_____

_____

_____

_____

_____

What big choices have you made in your life that have greatly affected its course?

_____

_____

_____

_____

_____

What little decisions do you make each day that you think matter the most?

_____

_____

_____

_____

_____

A PRAYER

Father, thank You for giving me strength every day to make the right choices, even if it means taking the harder path. I pray for Your wisdom in my decision-making and for Your encouragement when life feels rough. I know You are always with me. In Jesus's name, amen.

DAY 2:
THE ROOT OF OUR INTENTIONS

SCRIPTURE READINGS

MATTHEW 7:15–20 (NLT)

Beware of false prophets who come disguised as harmless sheep but are really vicious wolves. You can identify them by their fruit, that is, by the way they act. Can you pick grapes from thornbushes, or figs from thistles? A good tree produces good fruit, and a bad tree produces bad fruit. A good tree can't produce bad fruit, and a bad tree can't produce good fruit. So every tree that does not produce good fruit is chopped down and thrown into the fire. Yes, just as you can identify a tree by its fruit, so you can identify people by their actions.

LUKE 6:43–45 (NLT)

A good tree can't produce bad fruit, and a bad tree can't produce good fruit. A tree is identified by its fruit. Figs are never gathered from thornbushes, and grapes are not picked from bramble bushes. A good person produces good things from the treasury of a good heart, and an evil person produces evil things from the treasury of an evil heart. What you say flows from what is in your heart.

LIFE LESSONS

The reality of false prophets was well-known in Jesus's time. The Jewish people had been explicitly warned about them. A false prophet may look the part of an honorable person and speak the language of faith. They may seem righteous and exhibit extensive knowledge. They may speak eloquently and with a sense of authority. They may even believe they're on the right track (like the religious leaders in Jesus's time), but they end up misleading people.

If our intentions flow from the heart, and if what we say flows from the heart, then anyone who seeks to guide others to Jesus needs a heart that reflects Jesus. Their life needs to be rooted in Christ. You can't give what you don't have. A person whose heart is absorbed with power or fame might not even realize how they're influencing others who are observing them and listening to what they are saying. Such a person might do more harm than good, even if they don't intend it.

A person whose life is rooted in Christ will point people toward Christ. You'll see this worked out in how their life changes others for the better. Jesus will be present in their words and their actions. Take a look at those around you and use wisdom regarding the individuals whom you choose to look up to, because being around people who bear good fruit can make a huge difference in your journey and in your own ability to produce good fruit as well.

WHERE ARE YOU?

Name someone in your life who has exhibited good fruit. In what way(s) did they exhibit this fruit?

_____

_____

_____

_____

_____

Can you think of anyone whom you believe has exhibited bad fruit? In what way(s) did they exhibit this bad fruit?

_____

_____

_____

_____

_____

What kind of fruit do you believe you've been bearing lately? Can you give any examples?

_____

_____

_____

_____

_____

A PRAYER

Lord, may my life be rooted in my relationship with You. Guide me to leaders who are truly following You. Help me to produce good fruit and let my life reflect You in all I do and say. In Jesus's name, amen.

DAY 3:
JESUS DESIRES RELATIONSHIP

SCRIPTURE READINGS

MATTHEW 7:21–23 (NLT)

Not everyone who calls out to me, "Lord! Lord!" will enter the Kingdom of Heaven. Only those who actually do the will of my Father in heaven will enter. On judgment day many will say to me, "Lord! Lord! We prophesied in your name and cast out demons in your name and performed many miracles in your name." But I will reply, "I never knew you. Get away from me, you who break God's laws."

LUKE 6:46; 13:25–27 (NLT)

*So why do you keep calling me "Lord, Lord!" when you don't do what I say?…
When the master of the house has locked the door, it will be too late. You will stand outside knocking and pleading, "Lord, open the door for us!" But he will reply, "I don't know you or where you come from." Then you will say, "But we ate and drank with you, and you taught in our streets." And he will reply, "I tell you, I don't know you or where you come from. Get away from me, all you who do evil."*

LIFE LESSONS

It's possible to go to church regularly, raise our hands in worship, volunteer to work at the covered-dish dinner, attend countless Bible studies, and still not know Christ at all. It's possible to speak in front of thousands, making rousing speeches that motivate people to action, but not have a personal relationship with Jesus.

Yes, a person may do things in the name of Christ while having no real relationship with Him and experiencing no inner transformation. Performing good deeds or doing repetitive actions simply because we believe we *should* do them doesn't mean our hearts have changed.

Jesus wants us to know Him and be changed by Him. In these passages, He talks about people who did many seemingly great things for God, and yet He says He never knew them. They didn't spend any time personally with *Him*. A relationship with Jesus means a two-way street, not a one-way conversation.

Jesus doesn't care about our doing flashy miracles or leading millions of people at a time with a few well-spoken words. He wants us to be alone with Him, to get to know Him, to love Him. To have a daily walk with Him that impacts every area of our lives, not just a checklist of things to do and say. Those who truly know and follow Christ spend time getting to that place. They listen to Him and seek His heart. They know Him, and He knows them. That's the way He changes hearts and lives.

WHERE ARE YOU?

How much time do you spend with the people you're closest to? What impact do those relationships have on your life?

_____
_____
_____
_____

How much time do you spend per week getting closer to God?

_____
_____
_____
_____

What could you do to pursue your relationship with Jesus even more?

_____
_____
_____
_____

A PRAYER

Dear Jesus, I want to know You more. Help me to seek You and truly know You, not just read about You or go through the motions of following You. Give me Your perseverance so I can follow Your will for my life. In Your name, amen.

DAY 4:
ROCK VERSUS SAND

SCRIPTURE READINGS

MATTHEW 7:24–27 (NLT)

Anyone who listens to my teaching and follows it is wise, like a person who builds a house on solid rock. Though the rain comes in torrents and the floodwaters rise and the winds beat against that house, it won't collapse because it is built on bedrock. But anyone who hears my teaching and doesn't obey it is foolish, like a person who builds a house on sand. When the rains and floods come and the winds beat against that house, it will collapse with a mighty crash.

LUKE 6:47–49 (NLT)

I will show you what it's like when someone comes to me, listens to my teaching, and then follows it. It is like a person building a house who digs deep and lays the foundation on solid rock. When the floodwaters rise and break against that house, it stands firm because it is well built. But anyone who hears and doesn't obey is like a person who builds a house right on the ground, without a foundation. When the floods sweep down against that house, it will collapse into a heap of ruins.

LIFE LESSONS

Every day, we are in the process of building a life from the things we do and say, how we spend our time, and with whom we spend it. Just as is the case with a house, there is one essential component that keeps everything else in our life steady: the foundation. It prevents it all from falling apart. Our foundation, what we build our lives on, has to be solid, not something that flattens or washes away when life's storms come, leaving us empty.

Jesus compares two diverse foundations—rock and sand—to emphasize how we should ground our own lives. Those who build their lives on a relationship with Jesus Christ are building on rock, which withstands the storms of life. Those who build their lives on anything other than Christ are building on sand, which shifts and sinks and doesn't last through the hard times.

Actions, accomplishments, and other efforts without the right foundation aren't enough to keep us steady all the time. Having a relationship with God will change our hearts, making us like Him and giving us His strength and hope, a community of believers to help carry us, and other tools we need to withstand the hardest of situations. Our lives will be hit by many storms, but only one foundation will always remain steadfast, regardless of the size of the storm: Jesus Christ.

WHERE ARE YOU?

What storms have you experienced in life that felt like they almost tore you down?

_____
_____
_____
_____
_____

What methods of getting through rough periods have you previously tried that didn't work? What have you tried that did work?

_____
_____
_____
_____
_____

How do you get through hard times now? Whom do you go to and what do you do?

_____
_____
_____
_____
_____

A PRAYER

Jesus, thank You for being with me in every storm of life. Thank You for always holding me through the worst of times. Help me to build my life on Your foundation. With You, I can get through anything. Help me to trust You at all times. In Your name, amen.

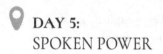

DAY 5:
SPOKEN POWER

SCRIPTURE READING

MATTHEW 7:28–29 (NIV)

When Jesus had finished saying these things, the crowds were amazed at his teaching, because he taught as one who had authority, and not as their teachers of the law.

LIFE LESSONS

When was the last time you heard someone speak who didn't just say words but embodied them? They spoke with passion, and there was a legitimacy to what they were saying that is rare. Hearing the words of such a person makes a huge difference, doesn't it? Those words impact you on a deeper level.

The word *authority* begins with the word *author*, and the New Testament refers to the authority of Jesus at least ten times. Jesus was able to speak with authority because He is the Author. He didn't passively recite phrases people had already heard at their synagogues or at the temple. His teachings weren't the usual instructions that had been engrained in them. He wasn't there just to impart some general wisdom but to express the fulfillment of the law. He didn't merely know the script, but He wrote it! He spoke *His* words into the lives of those around Him. And His words left people stunned. He was giving them new concepts, new ways of looking at things, spoken with the kind of authority that had the power to transform their lives—that has the power to transform your life…if you're listening.

WHERE ARE YOU?

When were you the most amazed (in a good way) by someone's words? Why?

_____

_____

_____

_____

Name someone you have listened to or seen whom you believe genuinely speaks with authority. What impact has that person made on your perspectives, attitudes, or actions?

_____

_____

_____

_____

_____

What kind of authority do your own words carry?

_____

_____

_____

_____

A PRAYER

Jesus, thank You for coming all the way to earth to speak to us in person and share Your heart with us. Thank You for the life You lived and for Your words to us. I pray that my life will continue to be changed by You. In Your name, amen.

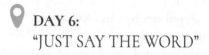

DAY 6:
"JUST SAY THE WORD"

SCRIPTURE READING

MATTHEW 8:1, 5–13 (NIV)

When Jesus came down from the mountainside, large crowds followed him....

When Jesus had entered Capernaum, a centurion came to him, asking for help. "Lord," he said, "my servant lies at home paralyzed, suffering terribly." Jesus said to him, "Shall I come and heal him?"

The centurion replied, "Lord, I do not deserve to have you come under my roof. But just say the word, and my servant will be healed. For I myself am a man under authority, with soldiers under me. I tell this one, 'Go,' and he goes; and that one, 'Come,' and he comes. I say to my servant, 'Do this,' and he does it."

When Jesus heard this, he was amazed and said to those following him, "Truly I tell you, I have not found anyone in Israel with such great faith. I say to you that many will come from the east and the west, and will take their places at the feast with Abraham, Isaac and Jacob in the kingdom of heaven. But the subjects of the kingdom will be thrown outside, into the darkness, where there will be weeping and gnashing of teeth." Then Jesus said to the centurion, "Go! Let it be done just as you believed it would." And his servant was healed at that moment.

SEE ALSO: LUKE 7:1–10

LIFE LESSONS

The centurion's absolute assurance in Jesus's power is remarkable. Can you remember a time when you were *that* sure of anything? This man has so much faith. He doesn't care what anyone else thinks or that he's not Jewish. He absolutely believes in Jesus's ability to heal. Even Jesus marvels at the man's faith.

The officer understands what true authority is: the ability to command without question and cause whatever is being commanded to *happen*. The centurion's own words commanded soldiers and servants, and he correctly deduces that Jesus's words have that kind of authority, too, but an even *greater* authority: one over the natural world—over sickness, over life and death.

Faith means trusting Christ's authority, His power—even if you feel like an outsider with God, even if you didn't grow up in the church or a Christian family, even if your relationship with Christ was on the rocks for a while. This man hadn't even been waiting for Israel's Messiah to appear, and yet his faith was greater than that of anyone Jesus had encountered among His own people. God answers our prayers of faith, regardless of where we are on the journey with Him. And His answers will be the right ones for our lives. Always.

WHERE ARE YOU?

How do you feel your faith compares to that of this Roman officer, and why?

_____

_____

_____

_____

_____

Has there been a time when you asked God for something, and you knew that He was working on it immediately? If so, what role did your faith play in it?

_____

_____

_____

_____

_____

What kinds of things do you usually ask God for? Do you ask them with full confidence in His ability to answer? Why or why not?

_____

_____

_____

_____

_____

A PRAYER

God, thank You for answering prayer. Help me to trust in You more today. Help me to overcome any doubts I may have about Your authority and power so that my faith in You can grow day by day. In Jesus's name, amen.

DAY 7:
COMING BACK TO LIFE

SCRIPTURE READING

LUKE 7:11–17 (MSG)

Not long after that, Jesus went to the village Nain. His disciples were with him, along with quite a large crowd. As they approached the village gate, they met a funeral procession—a woman's only son was being carried out for burial. And the mother was a widow. When Jesus saw her, his heart broke. He said to her, "Don't cry." Then he went over and touched the coffin. The pallbearers stopped. He said, "Young man, I tell you: Get up." The dead son sat up and began talking. Jesus presented him to his mother.

They all realized they were in a place of holy mystery, that God was at work among them. They were quietly worshipful—and then noisily grateful, calling out among themselves, "God is back, looking to the needs of his people!" The news of Jesus spread all through the country.

LIFE LESSONS

Can you imagine being the mother in this situation? One second, it feels like your life is over, but in the next, it's as though your life has just begun. Jesus's power transcends life and death, and His compassion covers us all. When He tells the widow not to cry, He's telling her to have hope in what's to follow. He's promising that better things are coming, because He's here for us, He loves us, and He has a plan.

Jesus holds the power of resurrection, and He displayed it, of all places, at a funeral procession. There is no greater shift than going from mourning death to celebrating resurrection power and life in a matter of seconds. And it's not just power over life and death that Jesus holds; He can restore us in other ways too. Dead things come to life in the presence of Jesus!

So, hold on to hope. Hold on to your knowledge of Jesus's power. Be ready for remarkable things to happen in your life. Jesus is compassionate, loving, and more than capable of turning our mourning into joy, of restoring us so that we are truly living.

WHERE ARE YOU?

What is the most remarkable thing you've ever seen?

_____

_____

_____

_____

Has there been a time when you asked God to do something, and then it happened? What were the circumstances?

_____

_____

_____

_____

In what ways do you need restoration today? How will you entrust those areas to Jesus and His love?

_____

_____

_____

_____

A PRAYER

Jesus, You are the Resurrection and the Life. Thank You for restoring hope to us when it has been lost, and transforming lives in so many ways. I am in awe of Your incredible power. Help me to live each day aware of Your power to bring life, both physically and spiritually. In Your name, amen.

DAY 8:
SINKING INTO UNCERTAINTY

SCRIPTURE READING

MATTHEW 11:2–6 (MSG)

John [the Baptist], meanwhile, had been locked up in prison. When he got wind of what Jesus was doing, he sent his own disciples to ask, "Are you the One we've been expecting, or are we still waiting?" Jesus told them, "Go back and tell John what's going on: The blind see, the lame walk, lepers are cleansed, the deaf hear, the dead are raised, the wretched of the earth learn that God is on their side. Is this what you were expecting? Then count yourselves most blessed!"

SEE ALSO: LUKE 7:18–23

LIFE LESSONS

We may go through seasons in our lives when we find ourselves slowly sinking into uncertainty. The uncertainty leads to questioning and then perhaps even to full-on doubt. This is especially true when we can't see the larger picture of what God is doing. Even people with the strongest faith sometimes fall prey to doubt. At times, circumstances can speak louder than our faith.

John had waited his whole life for the Messiah's appearance. He had preached repentance and prepared the way for Jesus, and now Jesus hadn't done what John thought He would do. John was sitting in chains in a prison cell, and none of the promised retribution against Israel's enemies had fallen on any heads yet. Rome was still in charge, and nothing had changed…the renewal of the world hadn't happened.

John had been the one to baptize Jesus; he'd seen the Father's confirmation of His Son when the Spirit descended upon Him. He'd heard about Jesus's later miracles and teachings. But when he didn't see the results he expected, doubt began to sink in. With our own lens of limited knowledge, when we are stuck in situations where we can't see what's next, it's not hard to fall into questioning God. Fortunately, we have communities to point us right back to Him. We have friends who can remind us that the present isn't everything, and can help us to put things into perspective again. Jesus sent John's disciples back to him to remind John that there were multiple prophecies to fulfill, that there was a lot more going on than John could see.

At that time, God's plan was still in the process of being revealed, and His plans for us can't be sped up either—they will be revealed in His perfect timing. In the meantime, our community is there to encourage us to keep going and to offer insight while we wait.

WHERE ARE YOU?

Describe some instances when you have doubted God because you couldn't see the bigger picture. What were the circumstances that made you doubt Him?

_____

_____

_____

_____

_____

Who supported you through your doubts? How did they help you overcome them?

_____

_____

_____

_____

_____

If you are still struggling with these doubts, who might you turn to—such as Christian friends, your pastor or another mentor, or your church family—to support you in the midst of them?

_____

_____

_____

_____

_____

A PRAYER

Jesus, You have a plan for me. It's bigger than anything I can imagine, and it will be revealed in Your own time. Please help me to focus on You instead of on my current problems. When I'm struggling, help me to seek out my community of faith and be open to their insights. In Your name, amen.

DAY 9:
OUR OWN WALK

SCRIPTURE READING
....

LUKE 7:24–35 (NLT)

After John's disciples left, Jesus began talking about him to the crowds. "What kind of man did you go into the wilderness to see? Was he a weak reed, swayed by every breath of wind? Or were you expecting to see a man dressed in expensive clothes? No, people who wear beautiful clothes and live in luxury are found in palaces. Were you looking for a prophet? Yes, and he is more than a prophet. John is the man to whom the Scriptures refer when they say,

> *'Look, I am sending my messenger ahead of you,*
> *and he will prepare your way before you.'*

I tell you, of all who have ever lived, none is greater than John. Yet even the least person in the Kingdom of God is greater than he is!"

When they heard this, all the people—even the tax collectors—agreed that God's way was right, for they had been baptized by John. But the Pharisees and experts in religious law rejected God's plan for them, for they had refused John's baptism.

"To what can I compare the people of this generation?" Jesus asked. "How can I describe them? They are like children playing a game in the public square. They complain to their friends,

> *'We played wedding songs,*
> *and you didn't dance,*
> *so we played funeral songs,*
> *and you didn't weep.'*

For John the Baptist didn't spend his time eating bread or drinking wine, and you say, 'He's possessed by a demon.' The Son of Man, on the other hand, feasts and drinks, and you say, 'He's a glutton and a drunkard, and a friend of tax collectors and other sinners!' But wisdom is shown to be right by the lives of those who follow it."

SEE ALSO: MATTHEW 11:7–19

LIFE LESSONS

No one has quite the same Christian journey as anyone else. We each have a unique purpose, and God will guide us differently as our purposes are fulfilled in distinct ways. On top of that, we each have different ways of expressing our faith and love for other people.

John the Baptist was instrumental in preparing the people of Israel for Jesus's coming. He trusted God, he fulfilled his purpose with his choices and actions, and he rejected the traditions of the major teachers of the law. In place of their teachings, which revolved around rules, John taught repentance. And he did it while wearing animal skins in the wilderness! But the religious leaders rejected his message entirely and called him crazy because of his lifestyle and approach.

Meanwhile, Jesus was dining with tax collectors, attending weddings, and also preaching a message the religious leaders refused to accept. So, these leaders made negative comments about Him, too. Despite Jesus's perfection, the teachers of the law didn't like His lifestyle either. In response, Jesus compared them to children who want everyone to play the game their way, even when they keep changing the rules.

Again, we all have our own walk with God according to His will for our lives. Yours might not make sense to someone else. It doesn't have to. What's most important—at the heart of it all—is salvation. Our paths and our processes will be unique, but they'll all lead us to Jesus.

WHERE ARE YOU?

What is your favorite unique thing about yourself?

How do you feel your walk with God has been distinct from other people's?

_____

_____

_____

_____

_____

Can you think of someone you really respect in your community who has a different way of showing God's love from your way?

_____

_____

_____

_____

_____

A PRAYER

Lord Jesus, thank You for the greatest gift of all—the gift of salvation. I know my path to fulfilling Your will for my life will be my own, as You lead me. Others will have their own processes. Remind me that my focus should stay on You and my relationship with You. In Your name, amen.

DAY 10:
GRATEFUL IN RECOGNITION

SCRIPTURE READING

LUKE 7:36–50 (CEV)

A Pharisee invited Jesus to have dinner with him. So Jesus went to the Pharisee's home and got ready to eat.

When a sinful woman in that town found out that Jesus was there, she bought an expensive bottle of perfume. Then she came and stood behind Jesus. She cried and started washing his feet with her tears and drying them with her hair. The woman kissed his feet and poured the perfume on them.

The Pharisee who had invited Jesus saw this and said to himself, "If this man really were a prophet, he would know what kind of woman is touching him! He would know that she is a sinner."

Jesus said to the Pharisee, "Simon, I have something to say to you."

"Teacher, what is it?" Simon replied.

Jesus told him, "Two people were in debt to a moneylender. One of them owed him 500 silver coins, and the other owed him 50. Since neither of them could pay him back, the moneylender said that they didn't have to pay him anything. Which one of them will like him more?"

Simon answered, "I suppose it would be the one who had owed more and didn't have to pay it back."

"You are right," Jesus said.

He turned toward the woman and said to Simon, "Have you noticed this woman? When I came into your home, you didn't give me any water so I could wash my feet. But she has washed my feet with her tears and dried them with her hair. You didn't greet me with a kiss, but from the time I came in, she has not stopped kissing my feet. You didn't even pour olive oil on my head, but she has poured expensive perfume on my feet. So I tell you that all her sins are forgiven, and that is why she has shown great love. But anyone who has been forgiven for only a little will show only a little love."

Then Jesus said to the woman, "Your sins are forgiven."

Some other guests started saying to one another, "Who is this who dares to forgive sins?"

But Jesus told the woman, "Because of your faith, you are now saved. May God give you peace!"

LIFE LESSONS

When we receive something from someone without seeing our need for it, we tend to be less grateful toward them. We don't take the gift seriously, and it doesn't affect our lives as much. A similar result can happen in our relationship with Jesus. He meets us where we are, but if we aren't in a place where we recognize our need for Him, we can easily brush Him off.

This woman offered Jesus overwhelming love and appreciation in her thankfulness for His forgiveness. The particular ointment she used could have been sold for the equivalent of three hundred days' worth of wages—approaching a full-year's salary! And onlookers were *rattled* by her actions.

On the other hand, Simon the Pharisee did nothing to welcome Jesus. In fact, he didn't show any appreciation for Him whatsoever. Sure, he showed a bit of curiosity and respect, but he didn't see in Jesus what the woman saw. This "righteous" man didn't recognize his need for Jesus, his need for forgiveness. And because of that, he didn't go out of his way to show gratitude to Him.

Every single one of us needs what Jesus offers. Regardless of our upbringing and actions, both good and bad, we need Him and the work of salvation and transformation He can do in our lives. Yes, it might be easier for someone who is desperate to truly appreciate Jesus's forgiveness on a deeper level because they can see how they have been forgiven for so much! But we are all in need of God's forgiveness and grace, regardless of our position in life. We all should stand back and be sure to recognize and exalt what Jesus has done for us and others.

WHERE ARE YOU?

Who stands out in your mind as someone you had to forgive after they hurt or wronged you? How were you able to forgive them?

When have you hoped someone would forgive you for something you did wrong?

_____

_____

_____

_____

_____

How can you better acknowledge before God your need for Jesus's salvation and transformation? How can you express your gratitude to Him for all He has done for you?

_____

_____

_____

_____

_____

A PRAYER

Jesus, we are all born into this world with a debt of sin, and You canceled that debt with Your sacrifice. I pray that I would never underestimate what You've done for me or my need for You. May I always be thankful and never think that my good deeds, rather than Your sacrifice for me, are the basis for my forgiveness and right standing with God. In Your name, amen.

DAY 11:
THE MIRROR OF THE HEART

SCRIPTURE READING

LUKE 8:1–3 (MSG)

He continued according to plan, traveled to town after town, village after village, preaching God's kingdom, spreading the Message. The Twelve were with him. There were also some women in their company who had been healed of various evil afflictions and illnesses: Mary, the one called Magdalene, from whom seven demons had gone out; Joanna, wife of Chuza, Herod's manager; and Susanna—along with many others who used their considerable means to provide for the company.

LIFE LESSONS

Women have always played, and will continue to play, a vital role in the ministry of Jesus. In His day, in a society and time that devalued women, Jesus proved that He created all people equal. We are all the same in the eyes of God. The ground is level at the foot of the cross—a place where, in a literal sense, women physically gathered as well.

The women in today's Scripture reading were not religious leaders. They weren't influential in the temple. Some of them had recently been cured of disease or released from other hardships. Regardless of their backgrounds, they shared what they had and financially supported Jesus and His disciples. Every single one of them had been helped in some way and had decided to respond in kind by giving what they could. These women knew that putting their resources into Jesus's ministry would mean far more in the end than doling out those resources elsewhere.

A good mirror of the condition of our hearts would be to see where our resources are going. On what are we spending our money and our time? What are we supporting? Are we giving back with our resources, when we have them, in response to what Jesus has given to us? Are we helping anyone other than ourselves? And, just as important, are we supporting the equality of women in the church?

WHERE ARE YOU?

In what ways did the women who traveled with Jesus support His ministry?

_____

_____

_____

_____

How had the women become acquainted with Jesus?

_____

_____

_____

_____

How are you supporting your own community of Jesus-followers?

_____

_____

_____

_____

A PRAYER

Jesus, thank You for breaking down the barriers of inequality between people.
I pray that You will continue to break down barriers so that all people will
know Your love. I pray that women in my community will feel supported and
vital to Your work. Thank You for everything you've given me. Please help me
to use it to benefit others. In Your name, amen.

DAY 12:
OPEN TO THE POSSIBILITIES

SCRIPTURE READING

MATTHEW 12:22–30 (NLT)

Then a demon-possessed man, who was blind and couldn't speak, was brought to Jesus. He healed the man so that he could both speak and see. The crowd was amazed and asked, "Could it be that Jesus is the Son of David, the Messiah?"

But when the Pharisees heard about the miracle, they said, "No wonder he can cast out demons. He gets his power from Satan, the prince of demons."

Jesus knew their thoughts and replied, "Any kingdom divided by civil war is doomed. A town or family splintered by feuding will fall apart. And if Satan is casting out Satan, he is divided and fighting against himself. His own kingdom will not survive. And if I am empowered by Satan, what about your own exorcists? They cast out demons, too, so they will condemn you for what you have said. But if I am casting out demons by the Spirit of God, then the Kingdom of God has arrived among you. For who is powerful enough to enter the house of a strong man and plunder his goods? Only someone even stronger—someone who could tie him up and then plunder his house.

"Anyone who isn't with me opposes me, and anyone who isn't working with me is actually working against me."

SEE ALSO: MARK 3:20–27

LIFE LESSONS

An old African proverb says, "The same boiling water that softens the potato hardens the egg." In our Scripture reading, two groups witnessed the same miracle, and it triggered completely opposite responses.

Neither group denied that a miracle had taken place. Nobody could deny Jesus's power. But the state of their hearts led them to entirely different conclusions about where that power came from.

The crowd is open to belief. They are amazed by what they have experienced, and they let their hearts hope and accept the possibilities. The Pharisees, on the other hand, take their denial a step further than previously. They no longer just oppose the fact that Jesus has power, but they twist the whole idea to fit their own agenda, to not have to change their views—even if it means that complete nonsense comes out of their mouths.

The Pharisees' hearts were already hardened toward Jesus, and in this passage, the divide becomes even greater. They start calling His words out as evidence for what they already assume about Jesus: that He is their enemy. They use whatever they can against Him.

Hardened hearts usually become harder. Closed hearts squeeze more tightly shut. Arguments become battles. Small cracks eventually become uncrossable divides. We need to keep our hearts open and continue working *with* Jesus, continue listening to Him and accepting the possibility that maybe we're not always right, but He is.

WHERE ARE YOU?

Why do you think the crowd and the Pharisees had such different reactions to Jesus's healing of the demon-possessed man?

_____

_____

_____

_____

When have you seen a small conflict or divide rapidly become something much bigger? What caused that to happen?

_____

_____

_____

_____

Are there ways in which you might have been resisting Jesus or working against His purposes without having realized it was happening? If so, how will you realign your attitudes and purposes with His?

_____

_____

_____

_____

_____

A PRAYER

Lord God, please soften my heart so that I can celebrate all You are doing around me. Don't let me live stubbornly within my own limited mindset, refusing to see the work You are initiating right in front of me. Open my eyes to the possibilities in You and to Your strength and power present in my life. In Jesus's name, amen.

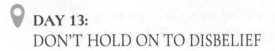

DAY 13:
DON'T HOLD ON TO DISBELIEF

SCRIPTURE READINGS

MATTHEW 12:31–32 (NLT)

So I tell you, every sin and blasphemy can be forgiven—except blasphemy against the Holy Spirit, which will never be forgiven. Anyone who speaks against the Son of Man can be forgiven, but anyone who speaks against the Holy Spirit will never be forgiven, either in this world or in the world to come.

MARK 3:28–30 (NLT)

"I tell you the truth, all sin and blasphemy can be forgiven, but anyone who blasphemes the Holy Spirit will never be forgiven. This is a sin with eternal consequences." He told them this because they were saying, "He's possessed by an evil spirit."

LIFE LESSONS

Every single one of us slips up sometimes. We say something carelessly. Think something awful. Make a bad joke and cringe when we look back on it later, or throw out a little "Just kidding, God, sorry," as we hope our comment didn't leave us destined for eternal damnation. (Come on, we've all thought it at least once.) But Jesus isn't talking about one-off slip-ups here, so put your mind at rest.

This is about our attitude. It's about not committing to God, refusing to fully accept Jesus, holding on to disbelief, and continually rejecting Christ with our words and actions. And, in this case, clamping on to these things to the point of attempting to discredit God's works entirely.

The Pharisees were present for Jesus's miracles. They saw them with their own eyes but continued to deny the source of Jesus's power. They continued refusing to receive Him for who He was. This persistence in not believing, in rejecting God despite everything, meant rejecting salvation *on purpose*. This was not an action of God. They did it to themselves through their own choices, over and over. Not only that, but in this passage they diminished Jesus, calling God's work Satan's work, and they ended up turning other people away, as well, twisting the purpose of Jesus's miracles and dragging others into resistance with them.

Still, despite the harsh-seeming lecture, Jesus offered grace. He gave them a warning but let them know they still had time. They could seek forgiveness. And why did He do that? Because He truly wants the best for everybody. He has compassion for us all, meaning He wants us all with Him, no matter how long it takes. (See 2 Peter 3:9.)

WHERE ARE YOU?

Do you feel like you're still holding on to any disbelief?

In what ways might your attitude or actions reject Christ's presence in your life?

How do you feel about Jesus's compassion—how He always gives more chances and more time?

A PRAYER

Lord Jesus, I praise You for being a God who wants all people to be saved. Thank You for continuing to seek me out, even when I've rejected You over and over with my words and actions. Please continue to remind me that Your grace is all I need. In Your name, amen.

DAY 14:
THE RESERVOIR INSIDE US

SCRIPTURE READING

MATTHEW 12:33–37 (NLT)

A tree is identified by its fruit. If a tree is good, its fruit will be good. If a tree is bad, its fruit will be bad. You brood of snakes! How could evil men like you speak what is good and right? For whatever is in your heart determines what you say. A good person produces good things from the treasury of a good heart, and an evil person produces evil things from the treasury of an evil heart. And I tell you this, you must give an account on judgment day for every idle word you speak. The words you say will either acquit you or condemn you.

LIFE LESSONS

The things we say matter. Obviously, we're not going to get it right all the time, but working on where our thoughts and words come from is what's important. If you find yourself wondering, "Why did that come into my head in the first place?" the answer is often, "It's what was in your heart."

There is an undeniable connection between your heart and your tongue. God describes our hearts as treasuries. In other words, our hearts store our thoughts and feelings for retrieval at a later time. What pops out of our mouths comes directly from what's in our hearts. As we grow in our relationship with Christ, seeking Him wholeheartedly and reading and obeying His Word, our hearts change. That reservoir inside us begins the process of being purified, and we become more like Jesus. Good things start to come out of our hearts—words of love, praise, encouragement…the list of positive and uplifting results could go on and on.

In this passage, these men's words were produced by cold, hard hearts—hearts that cared only about themselves. They couldn't wave off their comments as unintentional little mistakes. Their intentions were obvious. What was in their hearts was clear. It's not that they just needed to change their words. They needed to change their hearts.

WHERE ARE YOU?

What was the last thing you said that really revealed good coming out of your heart? When was the last time you said something you truly regretted? How do each of these instances reflect an aspect of your heart condition?

_____
_____
_____
_____
_____

Name someone in your life who always has kind words to offer.

_____
_____
_____
_____
_____

How can you better cooperate with God as your heart undergoes His process of purification?

_____
_____
_____
_____
_____

A PRAYER

Lord God, in Matthew 12:34 (NLT), Your Word says that "_whatever is in your heart determines what you say._" Help me to see my angry and hurtful words as a sign that my heart needs to change. Please fill my heart with Your thoughts and purposes so that the words that come out of my mouth will always be beneficial and loving to those around me. In Jesus's name, amen.

THE ONLY SIGN NECESSARY

SCRIPTURE READING

MATTHEW 12:38–42 (MSG)

Later a few religion scholars and Pharisees cornered him. "Teacher, we want to see your credentials. Give us some hard evidence that God is in this. How about a miracle?" Jesus said, "You're looking for proof, but you're looking for the wrong kind. All you want is something to titillate your curiosity, satisfy your lust for miracles. The only proof you're going to get is what looks like the absence of proof: Jonah-evidence. Like Jonah, three days and nights in the fish's belly, the Son of Man will be gone three days and nights in a deep grave. On Judgment Day, the Ninevites will stand up and give evidence that will condemn this generation, because when Jonah preached to them they changed their lives. A far greater preacher than Jonah is here, and you squabble about 'proofs.' On Judgment Day, the Queen of Sheba will come forward and bring evidence that will condemn this generation, because she traveled from a far corner of the earth to listen to wise Solomon. Wisdom far greater than Solomon's is right in front of you, and you quibble over 'evidence.'"

LIFE LESSONS

Many of us, at some point, have asked God to give us a sign. It's common for people to keep saying, "If God gives me a sign, then I'll believe." But do we really need another sign? And what happens if that sign we insist on seeing doesn't come? Does that mean we stop believing in Him?

The religious scholars and Pharisees asked for a sign despite all the ones they'd already witnessed. There was no good reason to ask for another, besides having a gesture made just for them—a test of God's power. But God doesn't manifest His miracles in order to prove His power whenever we demand it. He refuses to be tested. Instead, signs come in His own timing, given to us as gifts of grace.

These religious leaders had rejected all the other miracles already, so Jesus tells them that the only sign He would give them would be the sign of Jonah, referring to His death, burial, and resurrection. This is the only sign the world needs, even now, to know that Jesus is the Son of God. He doesn't have to prove anything else. He's already done it. All we have to do is accept that sign and believe.

WHERE ARE YOU?

In your own words, what were the religious leaders asking of Jesus? Why were they asking for that?

_____

_____

_____

_____

_____

Have you ever asked God for a sign? What were the circumstances surrounding that request, and what was your motivation for asking? What was the outcome?

_____

_____

_____

_____

_____

Do you know anyone who is waiting for a sign from God before they will believe in Him or trust Him? How might you pray for them?

_____

_____

_____

_____

_____

A PRAYER

Lord Jesus, thank You for the greatest sign of all, which proved that You are the Son of God: Your death on the cross and resurrection. You paid the debt that I owed. Help me to live my life with gratitude, not with an attitude of entitlement, as if You owe me something more. I already owe everything to You. In Your name, amen.

DAY 16:
FILLING THE INNER SELF

SCRIPTURE READING
....

MATTHEW 12:43–45 (MSG)

When a defiling evil spirit is expelled from someone, it drifts along through the desert looking for an oasis, some unsuspecting soul it can bedevil. When it doesn't find anyone, it says, "I'll go back to my old haunt." On return it finds the person spotlessly clean, but vacant. It then runs out and rounds up seven other spirits more evil than itself and they all move in, whooping it up. That person ends up far worse off than if he'd never gotten cleaned up in the first place. That's what this generation is like: You may think you have cleaned out the junk from your lives and gotten ready for God, but you weren't hospitable to my kingdom message, and now all the devils are moving back in.

LIFE LESSONS
....

When someone is newly sober after living a lifestyle of addiction, they're told to fill the hole left by the absence of the harmful substance with something else, something fulfilling and consuming. They still have a lot of brain space, time, energy, etc., that needs to be directed *somewhere*.

You can't just walk away from addiction and then sit around doing nothing. That would put the spotlight on what you're missing out on! You'd move through life keenly aware that it is no longer there. Life can't become a continual blank slate. Otherwise, when the temptation to return to that addiction comes back, and you have nothing to prevent it from taking over your life, nothing to protect you, the addiction tends to hit harder than before.

There can be a similar scenario in our spiritual lives. We may hear about God, get excited about His forgiveness, stop some of our bad habits, start going to church, help the homeless, and put money in the donation boxes but somehow never develop a relationship with Jesus. When we do this, we leave ourselves empty and vulnerable to worldly methods of solving that ache, that emptiness, in our soul. And people who turn to worldly solutions for their spiritual problems generally end up worse off than when they started.

Many people don't realize that even religion will leave you empty. They see external religious practices as a sign of an inner relationship with Jesus, but the two don't always go together. Those practices often focus on the outer religious self, while the inner self is left all alone. And when you're all cleaned out, there's space for anything to come in. Doing what seems like all the right things won't fill you, and cramming other fixes into your life won't mend you—but a relationship with Jesus will transform you.

WHERE ARE YOU?

In your own words, what is the lesson that Jesus is teaching in this passage?

_____

_____

_____

_____

_____

What does it signify that the former home of the defiling spirit is still empty?

_____

_____

_____

_____

_____

Have you ever tried to solve a spiritual problem with an earthly remedy? If so, what was the result? How might you have addressed it in a spiritual way instead?

_____

_____

_____

_____

_____

A PRAYER

Lord Jesus, I pray for Your presence to fill me—for You to fill me. I know You're the only One who can fulfill the deepest desires of my heart. Don't let me get comfortable just going through the motions, leaving You behind. Help me to constantly seek a deeper relationship with You. In Your name, amen.

DAY 17:
YOUR AUTOMATIC FAMILY

SCRIPTURE READINGS

MATTHEW 12:46–50 (CEV)

While Jesus was still speaking to the crowds, his mother and brothers came and stood outside because they wanted to talk with him. Someone told Jesus, "Your mother and brothers are standing outside and want to talk with you." Jesus answered, "Who is my mother and who are my brothers?" Then he pointed to his disciples and said, "These are my mother and my brothers! Anyone who obeys my Father in heaven is my brother or sister or mother."

MARK 3:31–35 (CEV)

Jesus' mother and brothers came and stood outside. Then they sent someone with a message for him to come out to them. The crowd sitting around Jesus told him, "Your mother and your brothers and sisters are outside and want to see you." Jesus asked, "Who is my mother and who are my brothers?" Then he looked at the people sitting around him and said, "Here are my mother and my brothers. Anyone who obeys God is my brother or sister or mother."

SEE ALSO: LUKE 8:19–21

LIFE LESSONS

Some of us grow up with supportive families who love us, those whom we can turn to and count on no matter what. Others of us aren't as fortunate. So, we create our own families out of those who truly care about us and are there for us when we need them.

As Christians, we're automatically members of another family altogether—a spiritual family. The Scriptures often refer to our relationships with God and other believers with familial language, such as "heavenly Father," "brothers and sisters," and "children of God." Now, Jesus isn't diminishing the importance of having an earthly family (we want to keep our relationships with our earthly family members strong, too, as much as possible), but He is elevating the importance of our spiritual family, our family of fellow believers.

When Jesus lived on earth, there were specific hierarchies both within society and within the various religious sects (such hierarchies can often be seen in society and in the church today as well). There was also a huge emphasis on family bloodlines. In these passages, Jesus wipes away the extreme significance of all that. He redefines how we should look at other followers of Christ and how we should treat and regard those around us who are also seeking God. We're all family. We're equal. In some ways, we are closer to other believers than we are to our physical family members (unless they are also believers). We share the same purpose. Our hearts are seeking the same Heart. We're called to support each other. Anywhere we gather in Jesus's name, whether it is in a home, in a church building, or out on a picnic, we are the church, and we are in this together.

WHERE ARE YOU?

What do these passages suggest about our relationships with other believers?

_____

_____

_____

_____

Do you treat your fellow believers as though they are family? Why or why not?

_____

_____

_____

_____

Do you feel that you have a supportive community of believers in your life? If not, how do you think you could join such a community or grow the one you are in?

_____

_____

_____

_____

A PRAYER

Father God, thank You for my earthly family. Thank You also for my family of friends who have supported me as I have gone through life. Thank You for my spiritual family as well. Help me to be supportive of and loving toward both my earthly and spiritual families. In Jesus's name, amen.

DAY 18:
SCATTERING THE SEEDS

SCRIPTURE READING

MATTHEW 13:1–9 (NIV)

That same day Jesus went out of the house and sat by the lake. Such large crowds gathered around him that he got into a boat and sat in it, while all the people stood on the shore. Then he told them many things in parables, saying: "A farmer went out to sow his seed. As he was scattering the seed, some fell along the path, and the birds came and ate it up. Some fell on rocky places, where it did not have much soil. It sprang up quickly, because the soil was shallow. But when the sun came up, the plants were scorched, and they withered because they had no root. Other seed fell among thorns, which grew up and choked the plants. Still other seed fell on good soil, where it produced a crop—a hundred, sixty or thirty times what was sown. Whoever has ears, let them hear."

SEE ALSO: MARK 4:1–9; LUKE 8:4–8

LIFE LESSONS

We all face moments when we're not ready to hear something. Wherever we are at that point in our lives—maybe it's because of the situation we're in, the fact that we haven't overcome a childhood trauma, or because we're just so certain of our own beliefs or perspectives—what we're being told can't quite penetrate.

Jesus often taught through parables. These were simple stories used to illustrate eternal truths, making them easier to understand. Some people refer to the parable in today's Scripture reading as "the parable of the soils." The soil here represents the condition of people's hearts and minds—whether or not they're ready to hear the truth and receive it. It's not up to us to judge anyone if they can't take in the truth right now, because, honestly, some people just plain aren't ready to receive it yet, for a variety of reasons.

Despite this, we can still spread the seeds of salvation to others through the example of our own lives in the way we love them, encourage them, and share how God has changed us. We can't save anyone ourselves. We can't force anyone to want God in their lives. Our job isn't to evaluate the soil or force it to change; it's simply to scatter the seed and give it the potential to grow.

WHERE ARE YOU?

How would you describe the potential of each of the four soils described in the parable?

Footpath:

_____

Shallow:

_____

Among Thorns:

_____

Good Soil (Fertile):

_____

How do you see each of these soils represented in the lives of people around you?

Footpath:

_____

Shallow:

_____

Among Thorns:

_____

Good Soil (Fertile):

_____

What type of soil would best represent your own life at this time, and why?

_____

_____

_____

_____

_____

A PRAYER

God, I pray for those who don't yet know You, that You would soften their hearts and prepare them to hear about You and receive You. Help me to be understanding and compassionate toward them, to never judge but instead to be an example of Your love. In Jesus's name, amen.

DAY 19:
LISTENING TO JESUS'S TEACHING

SCRIPTURE READING
....

MATTHEW 13:10–17 (NLT)

His disciples came and asked him, "Why do you use parables when you talk to the people?"

He replied, "You are permitted to understand the secrets of the Kingdom of Heaven, but others are not. To those who listen to my teaching, more understanding will be given, and they will have an abundance of knowledge. But for those who are not listening, even what little understanding they have will be taken away from them. That is why I use these parables,

> *For they look, but they don't really see.*
>   *They hear, but they don't really listen or understand.*

This fulfills the prophecy of Isaiah that says,

> *'When you hear what I say,*
>   *you will not understand.*
> *When you see what I do,*
>   *you will not comprehend.*
> *For the hearts of these people are hardened,*
>   *and their ears cannot hear,*
> *and they have closed their eyes—*
>   *so their eyes cannot see,*
> *and their ears cannot hear,*
>   *and their hearts cannot understand,*
> *and they cannot turn to me*
>   *and let me heal them.'*

"But blessed are your eyes, because they see; and your ears, because they hear. I tell you the truth, many prophets and righteous people longed to see what you see, but they didn't see it. And they longed to hear what you hear, but they didn't hear it."

SEE ALSO: MARK 4:10–12; LUKE 8:9–10

LIFE LESSONS

Not everyone shows up to church or Bible study to really seek God. Likewise, not everyone who sought out Christ to hear His teachings had pure motives. Not everyone joined the crowd because they wanted to believe in Him or were ready to do so. In the masses at large, many people came just for the spectacle, not to modify their entire way of living to follow Jesus. They didn't understand, and they didn't care to.

Jesus explained to His disciples that their spiritual understanding was a gift from God. It didn't come from their own efforts or natural talents. They were ready to hear and act on the truth, and their knowledge grew as they followed Jesus. At the same time, as many people in Israel purposefully and vehemently refused to accept Jesus, their hearts became harder and harder, and they gradually understood less and less. Jesus's statement was a fulfillment of the prophecy recorded in Isaiah 6:9–10. God had told Isaiah that he would preach, but those with hardened hearts wouldn't listen to the message.

One reason Jesus spoke in parables was to conceal the larger truth about what was to come from the people who refused to believe. They would have had to start opening up to be able to hear the message, so He let them continue down their path while trusting that those who were ready to receive would find the meaning hidden within.

WHERE ARE YOU?

Why was it important that Jesus spoke in parables at the time?

According to the passage, what would happen to those who listened to Jesus's teaching?

_____

_____

_____

_____

_____

What do you believe makes eyes and ears open to spiritual truth?

_____

_____

_____

_____

_____

A PRAYER

God, help me to keep an open heart and a willing spirit so I can understand more and more about You and Your ways each day. I pray for those who reject You over and over—that their hearts would soften and their eyes and ears would open, that they would recognize Your love and feel Your hope. In Jesus's name, amen.

DAY 20:
GOOD, TILLED SOIL

SCRIPTURE READING

MATTHEW 13:18–23 (NLT)

Now listen to the explanation of the parable about the farmer planting seeds: The seed that fell on the footpath represents those who hear the message about the Kingdom and don't understand it. Then the evil one comes and snatches away the seed that was planted in their hearts. The seed on the rocky soil represents those who hear the message and immediately receive it with joy. But since they don't have deep roots, they don't last long. They fall away as soon as they have problems or are persecuted for believing God's word. The seed that fell among the thorns represents those who hear God's word, but all too quickly the message is crowded out by the worries of this life and the lure of wealth, so no fruit is produced. The seed that fell on good soil represents those who truly hear and understand God's word and produce a harvest of thirty, sixty, or even a hundred times as much as had been planted!

SEE ALSO: MARK 4:13–20; LUKE 8:11–15

LIFE LESSONS

As we have noted, our hearts have to be ready in order to really take in Jesus's message of salvation and to keep learning from it as time goes on. Maybe the first time you heard the good news about Jesus, your heart wasn't yet ready to receive it. Maybe you just weren't interested. Your life was going well, and you were managing on your own—why bring a higher power into the mix? Or perhaps you know someone who was very excited about Jesus at first, but their enthusiasm lasted only a few months. Perhaps they didn't want to put in the work of being a follower of Jesus, or maybe making changes in their life turned out to be too much for them. Giving up our time, our habits, the things we hold on to…it's hard.

Different types of people hear the same message about the kingdom, yet they respond differently according to the condition of their hearts, how much interest they have, and how much they feel like they *need* Jesus. The seed that lands on good, tilled soil is the only one that produces a harvest; that soil represents the people who truly understand their need for Jesus and how absolutely irreplaceable He is. Realizing our need is huge. It's also vital in order to *continue* taking in Jesus's teachings, to continue to make those life shifts to align with His ways, and to know how worthwhile it all is.

Because of this, out of all the seed scattered, only a few seeds really land well and dig in deep. The difference among these seeds is the condition of the hearts on which they fall. Again, we can't drag anyone into truly hearing Jesus's message. We can't prep anyone's heart *for* them. We can only keep ourselves open and willing to continue seeking God and ensure that our soil stays primed to receive. And as our actions and lives reflect Jesus more and more, we will grow, and this will impact those around us.

WHERE ARE YOU?

In the parable of the soils, those who don't have deep roots end up falling away from God. What does it mean to have deep roots in the soil of your heart?

Can you give some examples of "thorns" that crowd out the good news in people's lives before they can really get going in their relationship with God?

How can you make sure that the soil of your heart is spiritually good and well tilled for the seed God sends?

_____

_____

_____

_____

_____

A PRAYER

God, I pray that I would continue to realize my need for You as time goes on. Don't let me fall back into focusing on the worries of life or give in to the lure of wealth and other things that can seem so significant now but don't last. I want my life to continue changing through You and impacting those around me for You. This can only happen through Your grace and strength. In Jesus's name, amen.

DAY 21:
A SLOW REVEALING

SCRIPTURE READINGS

MARK 4:21–25 (NLT)

Then Jesus asked them, "Would anyone light a lamp and then put it under a basket or under a bed? Of course not! A lamp is placed on a stand, where its light will shine. For everything that is hidden will eventually be brought into the open, and every secret will be brought to light. Anyone with ears to hear should listen and understand."

Then he added, "Pay close attention to what you hear. The closer you listen, the more understanding you will be given—and you will receive even more. To those who listen to my teaching, more understanding will be given. But for those who are not listening, even what little understanding they have will be taken away from them."

LUKE 8:16–18 (NLT)

No one lights a lamp and then covers it with a bowl or hides it under a bed. A lamp is placed on a stand, where its light can be seen by all who enter the house. For all that is secret will eventually be brought into the open, and everything that is concealed will be brought to light and made known to all.

So pay attention to how you hear. To those who listen to my teaching, more understanding will be given. But for those who are not listening, even what they think they understand will be taken away from them.

LIFE LESSONS

We don't turn on our bedside lamp just to throw a blanket over it. That would defeat the whole purpose of turning on the light! In the same vein, it makes no sense for the light of knowledge and truth, the Light of the World, to stay hidden. Jesus wasn't keeping some things quiet and speaking in parables without good reason. And He doesn't take His time revealing truth to us without good reason either.

Jesus wasn't yet revealing everything about the kingdom to everyone because there wasn't a need to. Can you imagine if He immediately told the crowds and the religious leaders the whole story of the things to come? He was *already* attracting opposition. Had He revealed everything, it would have resulted in an early end to the story. The leaders would have turned on Him even faster for who He claimed to be, despite having seen His miracles and heard His teachings. Even the people who had started to believe could only comprehend so much at once.

So, Jesus drew His message out, giving Himself time before revealing more, and giving other people time to receive. He shared small portions of truth about God's kingdom bit by bit so that people could understand these concepts. This was a message that needed time to grow. The same process is true for us. For the people who are willing to listen and change, God builds up their knowledge and their understanding gradually. He's not hiding anything from us. That would be silly. But the more prepared we come to Him each day, ready to follow, and the more we understand, the more God can show us. The more we seek His truth, the more His light will shine into our lives, making His words, His character, and His teachings clearer to us.

WHERE ARE YOU?

How well do you think you're listening to God?

_____

_____

_____

_____

_____

What are some things you could do to listen more closely?

_____

_____

_____

_____

_____

What is a truth that God has revealed to you over time?

_____

_____

_____

_____

_____

A PRAYER

Jesus, thank You for revealing Your wisdom to us over time. Please give me patience as I follow You, so You can show me more about Yourself, and I can build my knowledge and understanding of You. I want to be open to everything You have to teach me. In Your name, amen.

DAY 22:
WHAT'S ON THE INSIDE?

SCRIPTURE READING

MATTHEW 13:24–30 (MSG)

He told another story. "God's kingdom is like a farmer who planted good seed in his field. That night, while his hired men were asleep, his enemy sowed thistles all through the wheat and slipped away before dawn. When the first green shoots appeared and the grain began to form, the thistles showed up, too. The farmhands came to the farmer and said, 'Master, that was clean seed you planted, wasn't it? Where did these thistles come from?' He answered, 'Some enemy did this.' The farmhands asked, 'Should we weed out the thistles?' He said, 'No, if you weed the thistles, you'll pull up the wheat, too. Let them grow together until harvest time. Then I'll instruct the harvesters to pull up the thistles and tie them in bundles for the fire, then gather the wheat and put it in the barn.'"

LIFE LESSONS

You'll encounter many people in your life who seem like they're doing it all. They appear to have everything together: they're pious, they're involved in the church, they're vocal about their faith—but it's all a facade. You might never know, but they haven't invested at all in their actual walk with Christ. They refuse to undergo the radical, internal change that it takes to truly follow God.

The illustration in this parable is simple but poignant. The thistles, or weeds— which is the term used in certain Bible translations—represent those who don't have a genuine relationship with Jesus, and the wheat represents those who do—those who are actually listening to and obeying God and whose hearts are being transformed by Him. From the outside, the weeds and the wheat look exactly the same. The only difference between them is what's on the inside. Weeds are empty on the inside, while wheat contains seeds within that develop as the plants reach maturity. If there are weeds in the field, at harvest time, the wheat is separated from them.

God doesn't pull out the "weeds" among His people or expose them all right away. In this story, the farmhands might represent people who expect Jesus to sweep in and immediately clear out the weeds from the wheat. But that's not how God works. Jesus gives everyone the opportunity to turn to Him, allowing those who follow Him time to mature along the way. If you're feeling empty or as if your relationship with God isn't a real relationship anymore, this would be a good time to examine your heart, dive into some reading of the Bible and Christian books for insight and inspiration, talk to someone you trust about it, and put aside time for some heart-to-hearts with God.

WHERE ARE YOU?

Why did the farmer not want the weeds pulled before the harvest?

_____

_____

_____

_____

_____

Why is God not pulling out the "weeds" in the church in advance of the harvest?

_____

_____

_____

_____

_____

How do you feel you're maturing in your relationship with Jesus? What are some examples of that maturity?

_____

_____

_____

_____

_____

A PRAYER

Lord Jesus, I don't want empty religion. I want a genuine relationship with You that grows and matures over time. Don't let me fall into a mere routine instead of truly getting to know You. Help me to set aside the time and to put in the work that is needed for our relationship to grow. In Your name, amen.

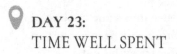

DAY 23:
TIME WELL SPENT

SCRIPTURE READING

MARK 4:26–29 (CEV)

Again Jesus said:

God's kingdom is like what happens when a farmer scatters seed in a field. The farmer sleeps at night and is up and around during the day. Yet the seeds keep sprouting and growing, and he doesn't understand how. It is the ground that makes the seeds sprout and grow into plants that produce grain. Then when harvest season comes and the grain is ripe, the farmer cuts it with a sickle.

LIFE LESSONS

Do your circumstances or the people in your life ever remind you that patience is a virtue? For example, when you start a new hobby or a new job, it can get rough when you want to be farther along in your expertise than you currently are. The time it takes for our skills to develop can be frustrating, yet there's nothing to do but learn, train, and invest our time in cultivating them, because we have no control over how quickly we or others can progress.

The same goes for our spiritual lives and the Holy Spirit's work in them. We can't see *how* He is working, and we can't force our progress to move more quickly. It doesn't matter if we're talking about our own walk with God or someone else's. Ultimately, we're not in control. Spiritual maturity happens in His timing. In the meantime, all we can do is trust in God and remain faithful to seek and obey Him.

As faith grows, it tends to show—although it can be hard to see for a while, especially when it comes to our own growth. But, eventually, we'll see God's character reflected in our thoughts and actions, and so will others. And we'll find that our time, despite how much it may have felt like we were stalled for a while, was well spent.

WHERE ARE YOU?

How patient do you think you are in terms of waiting on God and the development of your spiritual maturity?

Do you ever find yourself getting frustrated with the pace of your spiritual or personal growth and trying to force it? If so, in what ways do you try to do this?

What are some specific areas you can identify that show growth in your spiritual walk?

A PRAYER

Jesus, only You know how the Spirit is working in us. Give me patience when I don't see immediate results, when it feels pointless, when I feel down. I know I'll sometimes need Your encouragement and strength to keep going. Help me to not give up. In Your name, amen.

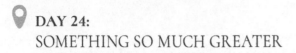

DAY 24:
SOMETHING SO MUCH GREATER

SCRIPTURE READINGS

MATTHEW 13:31–32 (MSG)

Another story. "God's kingdom is like an acorn that a farmer plants. It is quite small as seeds go, but in the course of years it grows into a huge oak tree, and eagles build nests in it."

MARK 4:30–32 (CEV)

Finally, Jesus said:

What is God's kingdom like? What story can I use to explain it? It is like what happens when a mustard seed is planted in the ground. It is the smallest seed in all the world. But once it is planted, it grows larger than any garden plant. It even puts out branches that are big enough for birds to nest in its shade.

LIFE LESSONS

Mustard seeds are tiny, only one to two millimeters long, but they can grow quickly and spread rapidly. They are almost weed-like in force. Jesus's message started off being shared between individuals and among small groups but quickly reached crowds and then masses of people. This is how the work of the Holy Spirit spreads. It begins as a small seed that grows in someone's heart and then spreads to those around them, continuing from person to person until the numbers seem endless.

We may feel insignificant at times, but we're part of something so much greater than we know. If you trust Jesus with your heart and seek His Word, God will grow you to new heights. But even at the start, when your journey is just beginning, God can still use you. Some people mistakenly think that their faith and their walk with God have to be at a certain level before He can use them. Not true. Remember, God is great at meeting people where they are and using what they already have. You're changing lives already and may not even realize it.

WHERE ARE YOU?

In what ways does a mustard seed aptly illustrate God's kingdom?

_____

_____

_____

_____

_____

How do you feel God is growing you spiritually right now?

_____

_____

_____

_____

_____

How have you seen God spread His message through your life and the lives of other believers you know?

_____

_____

_____

_____

_____

A PRAYER

Jesus, thank You for meeting me where I am and using my faith to impact others, no matter how large or small my faith is at the time. Help me to remember that I am an important part of something so much greater than I can see: Your eternal purposes for Your kingdom, which You are carrying out every day. In Your name, amen.

DAY 25:
AN EXPANDED HEART AND KINGDOM

SCRIPTURE READING

MATTHEW 13:33 (NLT)

Jesus also used this illustration: "The Kingdom of Heaven is like the yeast a woman used in making bread. Even though she put only a little yeast in three measures of flour, it permeated every part of the dough."

LIFE LESSONS

Have you ever baked bread? It doesn't take very much yeast (the ingredient that makes bread rise) when you're baking, especially in comparison to the amount of flour you have to use. A little bit transforms the bread from small, condensed rounds into large, spongy loaves. Just as yeast permeates dough and expands it, Jesus comes into our hearts and expands them.

As you continue to learn about God, yield to His will, and meditate on His Word, seeking to understand and apply it to your life each day, the influence and power of the Holy Spirit will spread throughout every area of your life. It is the same way with the kingdom of heaven—the spiritual realm over which God reigns as King. It begins in the hearts of individuals, then increasingly becomes larger and larger, expanding as the Holy Spirit permeates the lives of those around them, and continues to spread, giving hope and peace over time and space to more and more people.

WHERE ARE YOU?

In our Scripture readings, Jesus has been giving illustrations to explain the nature of God's kingdom. If you could choose your own simile, or comparison, to describe the kingdom of heaven, what would you say it is most like?

What is our part in inviting the Holy Spirit to permeate our lives?

_____

_____

_____

_____

_____

In what ways do you see Jesus working in your world?

_____

_____

_____

_____

_____

A PRAYER

Father God, it's amazing what You can do with small beginnings. I pray that the Holy Spirit would permeate my life and expand my heart so I can follow You as I should and spread Your love to others. In Jesus's name, amen.

DAY 26:
ONE PIECE AT A TIME

SCRIPTURE READINGS

MATTHEW 13:34–35 (NIV)

Jesus spoke all these things to the crowd in parables; he did not say anything to them without using a parable. So was fulfilled what was spoken through the prophet:

> *"I will open my mouth in parables,*
> *I will utter things hidden since the creation of the world."*

MARK 4:33–34 (NIV)

With many similar parables Jesus spoke the word to them, as much as they could understand. He did not say anything to them without using a parable. But when he was alone with his own disciples, he explained everything.

LIFE LESSONS

Introducing a brand-new concept to another person can be overwhelming. Taking in a brand-new concept can be even more overwhelming. Genuine understanding of anything takes time and some point of reference. If you throw a whole bucket of unfamiliar information at someone, they might miss the main idea, the essence, of what you're trying to tell them. They might get too caught up in the details, in trying to grasp everything at once.

Remember that Jesus used simple stories to illustrate larger truths one piece at a time. These small fragments of insight pushed for gradual changes of the heart and mind. They did not provide full details of what was to come, but rather *prepared* people for what was coming. Telling the crowds everything directly from the get-go wouldn't have allowed for that same understanding. It would have been too much for people to take in. Fully grasping something like this, accepting it, and walking it out wholeheartedly takes a significant change of perspective.

The Bible teaches that those who seek God will find Him. (See Jeremiah 29:13.) And, even in these passages, those who simply listened could find the truth. If there are things you don't understand, it's okay. God reveals knowledge over time so you aren't inundated by everything all at once. Trust in His process and keep your ears open.

WHERE ARE YOU?

Think of a concept that took you a long time to truly understand. What do you believe was the reason it took a while for you to understand it?

_____

_____

_____

_____

_____

According to the passage in Matthew 13, what is revealed in parables?

_____

_____

_____

_____

_____

Which of Jesus's parables that you have read so far has been most helpful to you in understanding God's kingdom, and why?

_____

_____

_____

_____

_____

A PRAYER

God, thank You for taking Your time with us, for preparing our minds and hearts for greater things. Thank You also for revealing Your wisdom and knowledge when we need it. Help me to trust in You when I don't have the answers or feel like there are pieces missing. Help me to trust that You are in control and will give me what I need at the right time. In Jesus's name, amen.

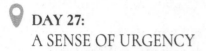

DAY 27:
A SENSE OF URGENCY

SCRIPTURE READING

MATTHEW 13:36–43 (NLT)

Then, leaving the crowds outside, Jesus went into the house. His disciples said, "Please explain to us the story of the weeds in the field."

Jesus replied, "The Son of Man is the farmer who plants the good seed. The field is the world, and the good seed represents the people of the Kingdom. The weeds are the people who belong to the evil one. The enemy who planted the weeds among the wheat is the devil. The harvest is the end of the world, and the harvesters are the angels.

"Just as the weeds are sorted out and burned in the fire, so it will be at the end of the world. The Son of Man will send his angels, and they will remove from his Kingdom everything that causes sin and all who do evil. And the angels will throw them into the fiery furnace, where there will be weeping and gnashing of teeth. Then the righteous will shine like the sun in their Father's Kingdom. Anyone with ears to hear should listen and understand!"

LIFE LESSONS

Once they were alone and away from the crowds, Jesus took the time to explain to His disciples in detail the meanings behind many of His parables. As we have noted, although Jesus may offer His instruction in bits and pieces or withhold something for a while when we're not yet ready for it, He wants to make Himself known to us so that we can follow Him completely and know Him fully.

Jesus says that when He returns in His second coming, there will be a day of reckoning. The angels will go throughout the world and remove *"everything that causes sin and all who do evil."* Like the weeds separated from the wheat in an agricultural harvest, everyone and everything that causes people to fall, that goes against God, will be gathered up, taken out of this world, and be subjected to God's judgment.

Knowing that we live in a world crowded with weeds, it does give us a sense of urgency to help those around us—to shine brighter, to be kinder, to be encouraging, and to guide with love. It's not about condemning people or forcing them to follow our instructions. It's about loving them and planting the seeds for their own change of heart.

WHERE ARE YOU?

In Jesus's explanation of the parable, who plants the good seed, and when is the harvest?

_____

_____

_____

_____

_____

How can you show more of God's love and shine brighter to illuminate His truth to those around you?

_____

_____

_____

_____

_____

Which truths stand out to you most from Jesus's teachings so far in your Life Along the Way?

_____

_____

_____

_____

_____

A PRAYER

Jesus, thank You for providing a way for me to be forgiven of my sin and have an eternal future with You. I pray that Your goodness and love will shine through me and bring more people to You. In Your name, amen.

DAY 28:
RETHINKING OUR TREASURES

SCRIPTURE READING

MATTHEW 13:44 (NLT)

The Kingdom of Heaven is like a treasure that a man discovered hidden in a field. In his excitement, he hid it again and sold everything he owned to get enough money to buy the field.

LIFE LESSONS

When we come across something life-changing, any sacrifices we may need to make in order to obtain it or to participate in it often don't feel like sacrifices anymore. We tend to go all out. We may move across the country, forgo our usual small luxuries, give up our free time, sell our possessions, or step out of our comfort zones entirely...because we know there's something much better waiting for us.

Being forgiven of our sins, receiving eternal life, and having a relationship with Jesus are the greatest treasures of all. In this parable of the treasure in the field, the man dedicates every effort to making sure he buys the field and acquires the fortune. He holds nothing back, giving up everything he currently has to obtain it. We all have habits, tendencies, relationships, and other things in our lives that may feel hard to give up when necessary. But if they're holding us back from seeking out the greatest treasure of all, it's probably time to rethink them.

The world and what it offers can't even begin to compare with Jesus and what He offers. What He offers us is better than any earthly thing we can find or experience, and it's time to get excited about that reality again!

WHERE ARE YOU?

What is the biggest change or sacrifice you've made for something you knew was worth it? How excited were you about what you knew was coming as a result?

_____

_____

_____

_____

_____

When have you recently found yourself excited by what you saw God doing?

_____

_____

_____

_____

_____

How does the prospect of eternal life with Jesus make you feel? What sacrifices are worth making to receive that eternal life and grow closer to Him?

_____

_____

_____

_____

_____

A PRAYER

Lord, forgive me for sometimes chasing after the things of this world rather than seeking after You. Help me to keep my priorities straight. I want to be excited about You again, ready to go all out for You. Remind me daily that my greatest treasure is in *You.* In Jesus's name, amen.

DAY 29:
A SEARCH AND A DISCOVERY

SCRIPTURE READING

MATTHEW 13:45–46 (NLT)

Again, the Kingdom of Heaven is like a merchant on the lookout for choice pearls. When he discovered a pearl of great value, he sold everything he owned and bought it!

LIFE LESSONS

Remember the story of the hidden treasure from yesterday's devotion, where the man sold everything he had to obtain that treasure? Well, Jesus felt the need to emphasize this sentiment again. It's so important to remember how valuable it is to enter into and live according to the kingdom of heaven. And not just that, but to understand that this takes commitment and effort on our part. How else do we expect to find hidden treasure? Or acquire the most valuable pearl?

Both of these parables begin with a discovery. There would have been no discovery without a careful search. By its very definition, a discovery generally denotes a search. The man discovered treasure in a field, but the treasure was hidden. It must have taken some effort to find it. The merchant was *seeking* the pearl. He knew there was a pearl out there that was worth all his possessions and more. It took dedication for him to keep going, holding on to the certainty of obtaining something more, something greater.

We, too, need to keep up the search—to keep going after God. If we seek the Lord with passion and fervor, we will discover that He is more valuable than anything else. Again, the sum total of all He is far outweighs the sum total of all this world has to offer.

WHERE ARE YOU?

What is the most valuable possession you own? If you bought it, what did it cost you to obtain it?

How do you keep this valuable possession safe?

What kinds of effort have you put into seeking God lately?

A PRAYER

Jesus, give me the passion to seek You fervently. I know that a life with You is better than any kind of life without You, no matter what it is. Give me the endurance I need to keep going in my pursuit of You, and help me to value You as much as You deserve. In Your name, amen.

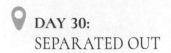

DAY 30:
SEPARATED OUT

SCRIPTURE READING

MATTHEW 13:47–51 (NIV)

"Once again, the kingdom of heaven is like a net that was let down into the lake and caught all kinds of fish. When it was full, the fishermen pulled it up on the shore. Then they sat down and collected the good fish in baskets, but threw the bad away. This is how it will be at the end of the age. The angels will come and separate the wicked from the righteous and throw them into the blazing furnace, where there will be weeping and gnashing of teeth.

"Have you understood all these things?" Jesus asked.

"Yes," they replied.

LIFE LESSONS

Even if you've never been out on a fishing boat and seen fish being caught in large numbers, you've likely seen footage of fishermen catching fish or seen a dramatic depiction of this process. There are entire TV series centered on fishing! Many times, when fishermen go out on the water and throw out their net, the net doesn't only fill with fish. It collects every object that is nearby those fish, and the fishermen bring all of it up to the shore, including pieces of old boats and other rubbish—whatever debris has been lurking in the water. Clearly, not everything in the catch will be usable, so the fishermen inspect and separate everything, saving the healthy fish and any other valuable items and tossing out the rest. That process is exactly what today's Scripture passage describes.

Matthew uses the phrase *"the kingdom of heaven"* roughly thirty times in his gospel. Again, this term refers to the spiritual realm over which God reigns as King. All people on earth are together now, regardless of whether they're sold on a relationship with Jesus. When the kingdom of heaven fully comes to earth, though, everyone will be separated—the righteous from the sinful. Let us remember that none of us can achieve righteousness without Jesus, without believing in Him and committing to Him.

WHERE ARE YOU?

In this parable, what represents the kingdom of heaven?

_____

_____

_____

_____

_____

What happens when the day's catch is brought to shore?

_____

_____

_____

_____

_____

What harmful or useless things might you need to separate out from your life so you can follow Jesus wholeheartedly?

_____

_____

_____

_____

_____

A PRAYER

Jesus, I pray that my life would encourage others to be ready for the day of Your return, that my heart would influence the hearts of others and turn them toward You. In Your name, amen.

DAY 31:
TRUTH IN THE OLD AND THE NEW

SCRIPTURE READING

MATTHEW 13:52–53 (NIV)

He said to them, "Therefore every teacher of the law who has become a disciple in the kingdom of heaven is like the owner of a house who brings out of his storeroom new treasures as well as old."

When Jesus had finished these parables, he moved on from there.

LIFE LESSONS

A lot of people today struggle with the vast differences between the Old Testament and New Testament texts. Even in Jesus's time, many people thought He was going back on or retracting the written Scriptures and replacing them with new concepts.

Jesus wasn't removing any value from the written Scriptures; He was building on top of them, showing what God was doing for us and altering the course of our futures. Although there is a definite shift between the two testaments, it's because Jesus came to earth to make that shift. None of it discounts what previously happened, though—the established Scriptures and the voices of the early prophets are still valid. Jesus introduced new perspectives that originated from the Old Testament writings because His work on earth *did* change our relationship with God. He *is* the change.

The way His coming happened in real time, the way He fulfilled the Scriptures, was drastically different from what many people expected. The people of God—whether they were disciples of Jesus, religious teachers, or average Israelites—had to reset their expectations for what the coming of God's kingdom looked like. And it was a hard reset. They had to figure out how to accept both the old Scriptures and the new teachings.

Becoming a disciple of Jesus enables us to see new value in what is written in both Testaments. It is one thing to know and teach what is in the Bible. But being a *disciple* of Jesus requires an open recognition and acceptance of the life adjustments that are needed in everything we think, say, and do in response to His teachings. Likewise, it is one thing to merely read the Scriptures; it's quite another to mine the treasures of truth within them and live according to those truths.

WHERE ARE YOU?

In today's Scripture reading, why does Jesus call the truths of the kingdom of heaven "treasures"?

_____

_____

_____

_____

_____

Have Jesus's words shown you anything new about the Old Testament or changed your understanding of anything in it?

_____

_____

_____

_____

_____

How have you had to reset your expectations of what it means to be a follower of Jesus as you have progressed in your journey with Him?

_____

_____

_____

_____

_____

A PRAYER

Lord Jesus, help me to be a committed disciple. Give me insight when I'm reading Your Word and living my daily life, so I can understand You better. Help me to adjust gracefully and with an open mind to Your plan and Your will when they're not what I expected. In Your name, amen.

DAY 32:
TRUST DESPITE THE STORM

SCRIPTURE READING

MARK 4:35–41 (NIV)

That day when evening came, he said to his disciples, "Let us go over to the other side." Leaving the crowd behind, they took him along, just as he was, in the boat. There were also other boats with him. A furious squall came up, and the waves broke over the boat, so that it was nearly swamped. Jesus was in the stern, sleeping on a cushion. The disciples woke him and said to him, "Teacher, don't you care if we drown?" He got up, rebuked the wind and said to the waves, "Quiet! Be still!" Then the wind died down and it was completely calm. He said to his disciples, "Why are you so afraid? Do you still have no faith?" They were terrified and asked each other, "Who is this? Even the wind and the waves obey him!"

SEE ALSO: MATTHEW 8:18, 23–27; LUKE 8:22–25

LIFE LESSONS

When was the last time you felt like the world was just plain coming down on you, like the walls were caving in? Maybe you couldn't pay your bills, you had a health scare, or you lost a friend. Often, when people end up in a dark place like this, instead of calling out to God, they panic. Their eyes get stuck on the problem and on their fear, and they frantically run around, not doing anything constructive.

When you find yourself in such a position—in that darkness, feeling afraid—how do you react? Do you reach out to God? More important, do you reach out in *faith*, knowing He's already in control of the situation?

The disciples had already seen Jesus do so much—heal diseases, cast out demons, raise the dead to life—and yet they still ended up in a frenzy when the storm got bad. They thought they were going to die, despite all Jesus had done before their very eyes, despite His promises that He had plans for them, despite the fact that it was far too early for Him to die (that would ruin all the plans), despite their trust in Him. The issue was that they didn't *entirely* trust Him. They hadn't even woken Him up to help. They had awakened Him because they were hysterical, thinking they were all on the verge of death.

Jesus never promised His followers a life of ease on earth, but He still expects our trust. Although the disciples had seen Jesus do so much, they hadn't seen Him control the weather or command the mountains or the rivers, so they assumed that would be impossible. They had to see with their eyes, once again, that Jesus was in complete control, that Jesus's plan would be fulfilled.

Jesus's authority covers even our external circumstances, not just our physical and spiritual selves. That doesn't mean everything will always turn out perfectly, but we need to know He's in control. The next time the world feels dark and stormy to you, trust that He is more powerful than the storm.

WHERE ARE YOU?

When things look bad, do you panic first instead of going to God?

Why do you suppose Jesus was sleeping in the middle of a storm?

Why do you think the disciples were terrified when they saw Him calm the storm?

A PRAYER

God, when life is dark and it feels like I'm in the middle of a storm, I pray that I would trust You and put my faith in You. You have control over all circumstances, and my life is part of Your greater plan. Help me to approach You with faith instead of panic. In Jesus's name, amen.

DAY 33:
NO INCURABLES

SCRIPTURE READING

MARK 5:1–20 (NIV)

They went across the lake to the region of the Gerasenes. When Jesus got out of the boat, a man with an impure spirit came from the tombs to meet him. This man lived in the tombs, and no one could bind him anymore, not even with a chain. For he had often been chained hand and foot, but he tore the chains apart and broke the irons on his feet. No one was strong enough to subdue him. Night and day among the tombs and in the hills he would cry out and cut himself with stones.

When he saw Jesus from a distance, he ran and fell on his knees in front of him. He shouted at the top of his voice, "What do you want with me, Jesus, Son of the Most High God? In God's name don't torture me!" For Jesus had said to him, "Come out of this man, you impure spirit!"

Then Jesus asked him, "What is your name?"

"My name is Legion," he replied, "for we are many." And he begged Jesus again and again not to send them out of the area.

A large herd of pigs was feeding on the nearby hillside. The demons begged Jesus, "Send us among the pigs; allow us to go into them." He gave them permission, and the impure spirits came out and went into the pigs. The herd, about two thousand in number, rushed down the steep bank into the lake and were drowned.

Those tending the pigs ran off and reported this in the town and countryside, and the people went out to see what had happened. When they came to Jesus, they saw the man who had been possessed by the legion of demons, sitting there, dressed and in his right mind; and they were afraid. Those who had seen it told the people what had happened to the demon-possessed man—and told about the pigs as well. Then the people began to plead with Jesus to leave their region.

As Jesus was getting into the boat, the man who had been demon-possessed begged to go with him. Jesus did not let him, but said, "Go home to your own people and tell them how much the Lord has done for you, and how he has had mercy on you." So the man went away and began to tell in the Decapolis how much Jesus had done for him. And all the people were amazed.

SEE ALSO: MATTHEW 8:28–34; LUKE 8:26–39

LIFE LESSONS

This man had a *legion* of demons possessing him. Not just one or a few. And these demons were ready to barter with Jesus to prevent from being sent out of the area. Notice that they didn't shy away from Him. They ran up to Him. They knew Him. Even the legion of demons recognized Jesus's power and understood He was in control. Do we?

Mark 5 has been called the "biblical home for incurables." Three cases are recorded in this chapter that were absolutely impossible to cure—humanly speaking. (We'll get to the others soon.) As we move through the fifth chapter of Mark, we discover that Jesus is more than adequate for every situation. He's all-powerful. There are no incurables with Jesus Christ. No matter what your history or your present situation, Jesus has the power to heal you, restore you, and set you free.

WHERE ARE YOU?

Was the demon-possessed man angry with Jesus, or did he want help?

Why did the local people want Jesus to leave after He cast out the demons from the man?

Have you known anyone who seemed incurable but was somehow cured? What happened?

_____

_____

_____

_____

_____

A PRAYER

God, thank You for Your miracle-working power. Help me to understand how vast it actually is, to trust that You can overcome *anything* that may come my way. Help me to focus on Your greatness over whatever problems may arise. In Jesus's name, amen.

DAY 34:
A DESPERATE FAITH

SCRIPTURE READING

LUKE 8:40–56 (MSG)

On his return, Jesus was welcomed by a crowd. They were all there expecting him. A man came up, Jairus by name. He was president of the meeting place. He fell at Jesus' feet and begged him to come to his home because his twelve-year-old daughter, his only child, was dying. Jesus went with him, making his way through the pushing, jostling crowd.

In the crowd that day there was a woman who for twelve years had been afflicted with hemorrhages. She had spent every penny she had on doctors but not one had been able to help her. She slipped in from behind and touched the edge of Jesus' robe. At that very moment her hemorrhaging stopped. Jesus said, "Who touched me?" When no one stepped forward, Peter said, "But Master, we've got crowds of people on our hands. Dozens have touched you." Jesus insisted, "Someone touched me. I felt power discharging from me." When the woman realized that she couldn't remain hidden, she knelt trembling before him. In front of all the people, she blurted out her story—why she touched him and how at that same moment she was healed. Jesus said, "Daughter, you took a risk trusting me, and now you're healed and whole. Live well, live blessed!"

While he was still talking, someone from the leader's house came up and told him, "Your daughter died. No need now to bother the Teacher." Jesus overheard and said, "Don't be upset. Just trust me and everything will be all right." Going into the house, he wouldn't let anyone enter with him except Peter, John, James, and the child's parents. Everyone was crying and carrying on over her. Jesus said, "Don't cry. She didn't die; she's sleeping." They laughed at him. They knew she was dead.

Then Jesus, gripping her hand, called, "My dear child, get up." She was up in an instant, up and breathing again! He told them to give her something to eat. Her parents were ecstatic, but Jesus warned them to keep quiet. "Don't tell a soul what happened in this room."

SEE ALSO: MATTHEW 9:1, 18–26; MARK 5:21–43

LIFE LESSONS

Have you ever been desperate enough to try *anything?* Did you have standards you held to, advice you avoided, or people you wouldn't listen to until your desperation became extreme enough to change your ways?

Jairus, the synagogue leader, must have known full well how negatively the other religious leaders viewed Jesus. But here he was, falling at Jesus's feet, pleading for help. Any previous reservations he'd had about the Messiah disappeared in the face of something very close to his heart. His daughter was more important to him than his religion and his religious position. He even brought Jesus home with him after hearing that his daughter had died. He was still putting his confidence in Jesus. He invited Jesus into his own house, throwing everything he had into believing that even the possible ruination of his place in the community was worth it because he believed Jesus was capable of helping him.

The woman with the hemorrhages had seen many doctors. She had known pain that she couldn't get rid of. Scholars say she was probably considered ceremonially unclean, so that touching Jesus would make Him unclean too. No one would have allowed her to do that. Still, she reached out anyway, against everything she knew to be acceptable, knowing full well the act could give Jesus the same stigma of being "unclean." And when she touched the hem of His robe, she was healed on the spot.

Will it take something drastic for us to finally show this much faith? For us to do *anything*, even if it means losing our position or being expelled from our community or family? And what if God does ask this much of us? Will we be willing to put ourselves out there and do it?

WHERE ARE YOU?

When did you feel the most desperate?

Why was it significant that the leader of a synagogue knelt in front of Jesus and asked Him for help?

_____

_____

_____

_____

_____

What do Jesus's responses in both situations—to the illness and death of Jairus's daughter and the affliction of the woman suffering from hemorrhages—teach us about faith?

_____

_____

_____

_____

A PRAYER

Jesus, I want greater belief. I want to genuinely believe You can do *all* things. I pray that I would be willing to put aside everything for You if You asked. Help me to be an example in my faith. In Your name, amen.

DAY 35:
STEPPING OUT BLINDLY

SCRIPTURE READING

MATTHEW 9:27–31 (NLT)

After Jesus left the girl's home, two blind men followed along behind him, shouting, "Son of David, have mercy on us!"

They went right into the house where he was staying, and Jesus asked them, "Do you believe I can make you see?"

"Yes, Lord," they told him, "we do."

Then he touched their eyes and said, "Because of your faith, it will happen." Then their eyes were opened, and they could see! Jesus sternly warned them, "Don't tell anyone about this." But instead, they went out and spread his fame all over the region.

LIFE LESSONS

It would have taken quite an effort for two blind men to physically follow Jesus and get that close to Him, especially with all the crowds going this way and that. Despite this, these men did everything they could to bring their greatest need to Jesus. They recognized Him as the Messiah from the stories they'd heard. They didn't have to see the miracles for themselves (as many did) to get to that point. They just believed. They believed enough to set out on the road, push through the crowds, and walk right into the house where Jesus was staying. And the eyes of both them were opened because of their faith in Him.

Would you follow Jesus blindly? Even when you were uncertain of where the next step would lead? Even if you hadn't yet seen Him working with your own two eyes? Do you think you'd have these men's level of faith and reassurance? Jesus has power over physical blindness, but He also opens the eyes of those who are spiritually blind. Have faith that He is working in you to increase your spiritual sight.

WHERE ARE YOU?

When have you gone above and beyond to find help for something you needed?

_____

_____

_____

_____

Name something significant (other than God) that you've believed without seeing it for yourself.

_____

_____

_____

_____

In what areas of your life and faith will you ask God to increase your spiritual sight?

_____

_____

_____

_____

A PRAYER

Jesus, help me to always follow You, no matter how difficult the journey becomes. Even in my moments of uncertainty, give me the strength to take my needs to You with determination and great faith. In Your name, amen.

DAY 36:
OUR EFFORT AND HIS WORK

SCRIPTURE READING

MATTHEW 9:32–34 (NLT)

When they left, a demon-possessed man who couldn't speak was brought to Jesus. So Jesus cast out the demon, and then the man began to speak. The crowds were amazed. "Nothing like this has ever happened in Israel!" they exclaimed.

But the Pharisees said, "He can cast out demons because he is empowered by the prince of demons."

LIFE LESSONS

People will always find ways to explain away the extraordinary and improbable things they see and experience. We do this to fit our own agenda—to save face, to feel good about ourselves, to not have to change our lifestyle, to secure our place in society. In this passage, the Pharisees see what's happening, and they know they don't have the same kind of power over demons that Jesus has, so they need a way around explaining His power while still rejecting Him as the Messiah. Their answer? Denying God's power in Him by attributing it to another kind of power.

We can get caught up in denying God's power as well, perhaps crediting only ourselves for getting through a rough patch or coming out of the dark fog of a toxic relationship. In the heat of the moment, we might see what God is doing, but once we are feeling better, we decide the positive outcome was all our own doing. Or maybe, after seeing someone else overcome what is physically impossible, we find ourselves praising only the resilience of human beings.

We tend to recognize our own contributions but fail to recognize God's. This isn't to discount our perseverance or struggles. We put in the effort. We put in hard work. But how many great moments where God has worked in your life have you minimized because of pride, thinking only of yourself and your accomplishments?

Today could be a good day to look back and start recognizing God's hand in your life. To start acknowledging His work in the midst of your struggles and hard times. To respond to His miracles with awe.

WHERE ARE YOU?

Why did the Pharisees accuse Jesus of being "empowered by the prince of demons"?

_____
_____
_____
_____
_____

What is the most difficult moment or situation that God brought you out of? How did He help you through it?

_____
_____
_____
_____
_____

What are some other situations where you may not have given God the credit He deserved for the help He gave? How will you give thanks for His help today?

_____
_____
_____
_____
_____

A PRAYER

Jesus, You are amazing, and I never want to lose my sense of awe at who You are and all You are capable of. Help me to recognize everything You do and have done in my life and in the lives of those around me. Remind me to give thanks where thanks are due. In Your name, amen.

DAY 37:
BELIEVING IN THE IMPOSSIBLE

SCRIPTURE READING

MARK 6:1–6 (NLT)

Jesus left that part of the country and returned with his disciples to Nazareth, his hometown. The next Sabbath he began teaching in the synagogue, and many who heard him were amazed. They asked, "Where did he get all this wisdom and the power to perform such miracles?" Then they scoffed, "He's just a carpenter, the son of Mary and the brother of James, Joseph, Judas, and Simon. And his sisters live right here among us." They were deeply offended and refused to believe in him.

Then Jesus told them, "A prophet is honored everywhere except in his own hometown and among his relatives and his own family." And because of their unbelief, he couldn't do any miracles among them except to place his hands on a few sick people and heal them. And he was amazed at their unbelief.

Then Jesus went from village to village, teaching the people.

SEE ALSO: MATTHEW 13:54–58

LIFE LESSONS

First the people are amazed, then they're offended. There's no way this childhood friend, this little boy from town who grew up alongside them, could have such power and wisdom. They knew Him from when He was tiny. How could this be? Whether it is due to jealousy or doubt, their insistence that it couldn't be possible makes it impossible for them to see what's directly in front of their faces.

Holding on to their past notions, dwelling on what their lives were like before, and harboring doubts—such practices keep many people from encountering God's miracle-working power. It doesn't mean God isn't working. It means the people in question might never *see* it—even if they physically witness it. Jesus continues to heal people at the synagogue, He continues to perform miracles, but these things don't count as miracles in the eyes of the people present. Once someone has decided something isn't possible, it's hard to turn their thinking around.

Doubt may hinder God's work in our lives or make us unable to see that He's working, but His power will still be present. When this happens, He's still involved and demonstrating His power, but we won't be able to process it. Again, when people decide something isn't possible, it will stay impossible for them. We need to believe in the "impossible" to see God for who He really is.

WHERE ARE YOU?

Have you ever found it hard to believe that someone from your childhood ended up influential or successful?

_____

_____

_____

_____

_____

If the people in Jesus's hometown were amazed at His teachings and miracles, why do you think they were also offended? What was Jesus's response to their reaction?

_____

_____

_____

_____

_____

What does this account say about God working in the lives of those who refuse to believe?

_____

_____

_____

_____

_____

A PRAYER

Jesus, You are capable of doing seemingly impossible things. Help me to notice Your miraculous acts—to truly see them. Remind me of Your power and Your involvement in my life. In Your name, amen.

DAY 38:
GETTING UP TO HELP

SCRIPTURE READING

MATTHEW 9:35–38 (NLT)

Jesus traveled through all the towns and villages of that area, teaching in the synagogues and announcing the Good News about the Kingdom. And he healed every kind of disease and illness. When he saw the crowds, he had compassion on them because they were confused and helpless, like sheep without a shepherd. He said to his disciples, "The harvest is great, but the workers are few. So pray to the Lord who is in charge of the harvest; ask him to send more workers into his fields."

LIFE LESSONS

The Savior of the world was also a servant to the world. Early historians estimated that there were over two hundred cities and villages in the region of Galilee during the time of Christ. Scripture teaches that in an area approximately forty miles wide and seventy miles long, Jesus went to *every* town and village.

As Jesus traveled, He saw how vast the need was among the people, and He felt burdened with compassion for all the lost souls. We should share the compassion of Jesus. There are so many people wandering around, waiting for things to make sense, to get better. Waiting for hope and guidance. It should pull at our heartstrings. How do you feel when you see the people in your community hurting, lost, and running in circles, looking for something greater for their lives?

Jesus gives us a little push here. In order for all these people to be helped, we need to get up and help them. We need more workers. We need more people to serve so others can find hope and stop living aimlessly. Jesus set the example for us, and now He's calling us to do the same. (Keep in mind, there are many different forms of serving others, so don't relegate this idea to a particular box.) Pray for more workers, but don't be surprised when you hear God asking you to get out there too!

WHERE ARE YOU?

What was the good news Jesus was preaching?

_____

_____

_____

_____

What does this passage reveal about Jesus's compassion? What does it say about what our lives and attitudes should be like if we're meant to be like Him?

_____

_____

_____

_____

In what way is the Lord sending you into His harvest fields?

_____

_____

_____

_____

A PRAYER

Jesus, Your love and compassion are endless. Help me to have a heart for other people and a willingness to get up and help them. Give me Your compassion so that I can continue to have a servant's heart even when it's difficult. Give me strength when it feels like it's too much. In Your name, amen.

DAY 39:
NOT FOR SALE

SCRIPTURE READING

MATTHEW 10:1–15 (NLT)

Jesus called his twelve disciples together and gave them authority to cast out evil spirits and to heal every kind of disease and illness. Here are the names of the twelve apostles:

> *first, Simon (also called Peter),*
> *then Andrew (Peter's brother),*
> *James (son of Zebedee),*
> *John (James's brother),*
> *Philip,*
> *Bartholomew,*
> *Thomas,*
> *Matthew (the tax collector),*
> *James (son of Alphaeus),*
> *Thaddaeus,*
> *Simon (the zealot),*
> *Judas Iscariot (who later betrayed him).*

Jesus sent out the twelve apostles with these instructions: "Don't go to the Gentiles or the Samaritans, but only to the people of Israel—God's lost sheep. Go and announce to them that the Kingdom of Heaven is near. Heal the sick, raise the dead, cure those with leprosy, and cast out demons. Give as freely as you have received!

"Don't take any money in your money belts—no gold, silver, or even copper coins. Don't carry a traveler's bag with a change of clothes and sandals or even a walking stick. Don't hesitate to accept hospitality, because those who work deserve to be fed.

"Whenever you enter a city or village, search for a worthy person and stay in his home until you leave town. When you enter the home, give it your blessing. If it turns out to be a worthy home, let your blessing stand; if it is not, take back the blessing. If any household or town refuses to welcome you or listen to your message, shake its dust from your feet as you leave. I tell you the truth, the wicked cities of Sodom and Gomorrah will be better off than such a town on the judgment day."

SEE ALSO: MARK 6:7–11; LUKE 9:1–5

LIFE LESSONS

Have you ever been sent on a work trip by your boss? Your employer probably equipped you for the trip—paid for your plane ticket, made sure you had the technology to give your presentation, maybe even gave you a credit card to take an important client to dinner.

So far, Jesus's disciples have stood back and watched Him work, but now it's their turn to go out to proclaim the good news. Those whom Jesus had just challenged to pray, He also called to become workers. And as He sent them out, He equipped them—but not in the way we would think of for a journey like that. He bestowed them with spiritual gifts and everything they'd been taught. They were to bring no money, no extra bag of clothes, no backup pair of sandals. They weren't to ask for anything either. They couldn't accept payment; they couldn't ask for payment. Hospitality was to be given and received freely, and God would provide for all their needs.

We don't need much in terms of material goods to share the gospel, and no one can buy their way into the kingdom of God. Salvation is not for sale. It was freely given by Jesus and will continue to be a gift. Anything else would skew the whole purpose of His message. This also means we won't become rich by worldly standards through sharing the gospel. To emphasize financial success would be a disservice to what Jesus did for us. Receiving what He accomplished is the same price for everyone—the price of changing our lives, not our pocketbooks. You have everything you need to be an example to others.

WHERE ARE YOU?

To whom did Jesus send His disciples? Why do you think He sent them to those particular people alone?

What message were the disciples to bring, and how were they to demonstrate it?

_____

_____

_____

_____

_____

When sharing the gospel, why is it so important not to emphasize financial success or buying one's way into God's kingdom?

_____

_____

_____

_____

A PRAYER

Jesus, thank You for the privilege of knowing and serving You. You have called us all to be examples of Your love and grace, to be light in a dark world. I pray that I would live up to that calling. Don't let me be distracted by what I don't have; instead, help me to remember all that I do have in You and through You. In Your name, amen.

DAY 40:
BALANCED AND READY

SCRIPTURE READING

MATTHEW 10:16–26 (NIV)

I am sending you out like sheep among wolves. Therefore be as shrewd as snakes and as innocent as doves. Be on your guard; you will be handed over to the local councils and be flogged in the synagogues. On my account you will be brought before governors and kings as witnesses to them and to the Gentiles. But when they arrest you, do not worry about what to say or how to say it. At that time you will be given what to say, for it will not be you speaking, but the Spirit of your Father speaking through you.

Brother will betray brother to death, and a father his child; children will rebel against their parents and have them put to death. You will be hated by everyone because of me, but the one who stands firm to the end will be saved. When you are persecuted in one place, flee to another. Truly I tell you, you will not finish going through the towns of Israel before the Son of Man comes.

The student is not above the teacher, nor a servant above his master. It is enough for students to be like their teachers, and servants like their masters. If the head of the house has been called Beelzebul, how much more the members of his household!

So do not be afraid of them, for there is nothing concealed that will not be disclosed, or hidden that will not be made known.

LIFE LESSONS

Sheep are defenseless animals, and wolves are their most dangerous predator. Through this analogy, Jesus gave His disciples a graphic illustration of the coming rejection and persecution they would face out in the world. Jesus's words to them here would not be fulfilled until after He ascended into heaven, but He was explaining the future of ministry for His disciples. He wanted to make it clear what the cost can be for true discipleship.

Jesus emphasized how we need to be ready in an appropriate manner. Not prepped to fight all the time but shrewd as snakes and innocent as doves. This isn't the easiest balance. When things become heated or we're unwelcome by others, He wants us to be perceptive, prudent, and informed. We're not to bowl over the people who oppose us. We shouldn't be screaming or whining at them, nor sinking to any kind of hatred. Instead, we should be an example to them, tell the truth, evaluate our situations with discernment, slip away when we need to, and maintain the soft, compassionate condition of our own hearts.

WHERE ARE YOU?

In your own words, what do you think it means to be "as shrewd as snakes and as innocent as doves"?

Have you ever faced rejection or persecution because of your beliefs? What happened?

How can we keep soft, compassionate hearts when we face hatred and rejection?

A PRAYER

Jesus, thank You for Your first disciples, who were willing to count the cost and pay the price to follow You. Because of their dedication, the gospel was proclaimed, and we have Your Word today. Help me to judge all situations with discernment, as You would. Give me wisdom and grace when I speak to others about You. Let my words and manner reflect Yours. In Your name, amen.

DAY 41:
YOUR FATHER'S CARE

SCRIPTURE READING

MATTHEW 10:27–31 (NIV)

What I tell you in the dark, speak in the daylight; what is whispered in your ear, proclaim from the roofs. Do not be afraid of those who kill the body but cannot kill the soul. Rather, be afraid of the One who can destroy both soul and body in hell. Are not two sparrows sold for a penny? Yet not one of them will fall to the ground outside your Father's care. And even the very hairs of your head are all numbered. So don't be afraid; you are worth more than many sparrows.

LIFE LESSONS

Fear isn't always a bad thing. There's a proper kind of fear that we should have regarding certain kinds of physical danger. It's more of a kind of respect, a knowledge of the consequences of falling into that danger, sometimes at an almost instinctual level. This is a healthy form of fear, not a cowering fear. The kind of fear with which we should approach God is similar: awe and respect for His greatness. He holds power and authority over this world and the one to come. When bad things happen, we cannot lose sight of this reality and of who God is and how He views us: we are valuable to Him. He knows every scratch, every scar, every freckle we have. And He is with us through everything.

In Jesus's day, sparrows were commonplace and cheap, yet, in this passage, Jesus points out that God still cares for them. God knows precisely when one is taken out of the sky. Similarly, He knows each one of us—each of the billions of people around the world—down to the constantly changing number of hairs on our heads. He is concerned with every detail of our lives. If it seems like He isn't answering our prayers, it's not because He's gone. He is always there.

This does not mean we will always be protected from harm, but when we face a person or situation that is troubling, we have a God who is fully invested in us and is so much more powerful than the situation itself. Acknowledge your fear but know that you are being taken care of to the end.

WHERE ARE YOU?

How would you explain "respectful fear," as described at the beginning of this devotion, to someone else?

_____

_____

_____

_____

_____

How does it make you feel to realize God cares about you so much that He knows how many hairs are on your head at any given time?

_____

_____

_____

_____

_____

Understanding your heavenly Father's care for you, what circumstance in your life can you entrust to Him today?

_____

_____

_____

_____

_____

A PRAYER

God, You know everything about me. You know when I'm scared, when I'm happy, when I'm upset, and when I'm excited. Things will happen in this world that I can't control, but I know You are with me every step of the way. Help me to keep this in mind when I'm afraid or when things look bleak. You are the only One who can truly save. In Jesus's name, amen.

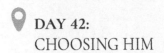

DAY 42:
CHOOSING HIM

SCRIPTURE READING

MATTHEW 10:32–39 (NIV)

Whoever acknowledges me before others, I will also acknowledge before my Father in heaven. But whoever disowns me before others, I will disown before my Father in heaven.

Do not suppose that I have come to bring peace to the earth. I did not come to bring peace, but a sword. For I have come to turn

> *"a man against his father,*
> > *a daughter against her mother,*
> *a daughter-in-law against her mother-in-law—*
> > *a man's enemies will be the members of his own household."*

Anyone who loves their father or mother more than me is not worthy of me; anyone who loves their son or daughter more than me is not worthy of me. Whoever does not take up their cross and follow me is not worthy of me. Whoever finds their life will lose it, and whoever loses their life for my sake will find it.

LIFE LESSONS

It's easy to walk around saying we love God, singing praise songs and lifting our hands at church. It's much harder to live a life surrendered to God. One requires a simple statement from our lips. The other requires complete surrender of our daily decisions, our time, and our resources—every aspect of our lives.

What does it say if you run away from God constantly just so you can do whatever you want? It probably means that your heart is not following Him and that you're not making the necessary adjustments to be like Him. God is asking for us to be fully with Him, to not deny Him, to not change loyalty when it suits us.

We are meant to choose God over everything and everyone else. This doesn't mean we aren't to spend time developing our human relationships, and it doesn't mean we don't love other people, especially those who are broken or lost. We are still made for relationships and are still to befriend others who are not like us, but we cannot let those relationships pull us away from total devotion to our Lord.

WHERE ARE YOU?

What does it mean to "acknowledge" Jesus before others?

_____

_____

_____

_____

_____

What have you had to let go of in your life in order to follow Him?

_____

_____

_____

_____

_____

How has your life changed for the better since you welcomed Jesus in?

_____

_____

_____

_____

_____

A PRAYER

Jesus, please help me to be consistent in my walk with You. I don't want to raise my hands in worship and then run to what's easy when the hard decisions arise. Help me to acknowledge You as Lord in every area of my life. Help me to always choose You. In Your name, amen.

DAY 43:
A SUPPORTING ROLE

SCRIPTURE READING

MATTHEW 10:40–42 (NIV)

Anyone who welcomes you welcomes me, and anyone who welcomes me welcomes the one who sent me. Whoever welcomes a prophet as a prophet will receive a prophet's reward, and whoever welcomes a righteous person as a righteous person will receive a righteous person's reward. And if anyone gives even a cup of cold water to one of these little ones who is my disciple, truly I tell you, that person will certainly not lose their reward.

LIFE LESSONS

We all have different talents, capabilities, backgrounds, and positions in society. We don't expect others to be able to do everything we can do, and vice versa. Just as we each play a unique part in the world around us, God has given each of us specific roles and responsibilities to fulfill His plan. These roles are determined by His giftings and grace.

God doesn't call everyone to stand in front of a congregation or to be on TV, speaking to the masses. He doesn't call everyone to pick up and travel across the globe to spread the good news. He calls some people to simpler, more everyday tasks, but these tasks are just as vital. One is not less important than the other. Each of our roles balances the others out so we can support one another.

A great example of this is in the story of Moses. Moses needed Aaron and Hur to hold his arms up high so that God could send the victory in battle. That was God's requirement to win. Every time Moses lowered his arms, the Israelites started losing, but Moses didn't have the strength to keep his arms up for as long as was necessary. The two other men supported his arms to ensure they could remain up until the victory was won. (See Exodus 17:8–13.) In the same way, we support others along their journeys.

Whatever your role, everyone receives the same reward. If you support someone who leads thousands to the Lord through preaching, it's as if you had preached every message yourself because your impact was actually that big. This is the beauty of each of us operating within our gifting. It multiplies our impact. You are just as essential to God's purposes as any big-name pastor or the person who gives their life to help those in poverty. You just have to figure out—through prayer, seeking God, and an honest assessment of your abilities—what you have to give and then use it!

WHERE ARE YOU?

In today's Scripture reading, what does it mean to "welcome" someone? What does Jesus promise us when we do that?

_____

_____

_____

_____

How does this passage emphasize even the smallest actions done in love?

_____

_____

_____

_____

What gifts and abilities do you have with which you can serve the Lord?

_____

_____

_____

_____

A PRAYER

Jesus, help me to serve You to the best of my ability in the areas to which You have called me. Don't let me compare myself to others. Help me to appreciate my own gifts, and open my eyes to ways I can support the people around me. In Your name, amen.

DAY 44:
A MESSAGE OF VICTORY

SCRIPTURE READINGS

MATTHEW 11:1 (NLT)

When Jesus had finished giving these instructions to his twelve disciples, he went out to teach and preach in towns throughout the region.

MARK 6:12–13 (NLT)

So the disciples went out, telling everyone they met to repent of their sins and turn to God. And they cast out many demons and healed many sick people, anointing them with olive oil.

LUKE 9:6 (NLT)

So they began their circuit of the villages, preaching the Good News and healing the sick.

LIFE LESSONS

In Luke 9:6, the phrase *"preaching the Good News"* comes from the Greek word *euaggelizo*. It is from this word that we get the English term "evangelism" for describing the witness and spread of the gospel.

Euaggelizo was a word used in the ancient world to pronounce victory over an enemy. When an army was victorious, a messenger would run from the battle back to the people and announce the good news of their triumph. It would be a time of celebration as the conquering city received word that the enemy had been defeated. Families rejoiced, knowing that they wouldn't be enslaved by their enemy. Victory had secured their freedom.

In this passage, the disciples similarly hurried out to tell people the good news. And they were giving a message of victory, news of freedom. Are we doing the same? It is up to us to make sure we are announcing the same good news—not an announcement of rules, exclusion, or fire and brimstone. This message is a celebration of life and hope and overcoming. It's a message of Jesus's victory over our captivity to sin and death.

WHERE ARE YOU?

In what ways is Jesus's message a message of victory?

_____

_____

_____

_____

Why is it so important how we share the news of Christ with others?

_____

_____

_____

_____

_____

How might you share the message of Jesus's victory with someone you know?

_____

_____

_____

_____

_____

A PRAYER

Jesus, help me to spread the *good news*—the victory and the hope that come from a relationship with You—with others. Thank You for making Your victory over sin our reality. Thank You for freeing us from our spiritual debt. In Your name, amen.

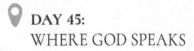

DAY 45:
WHERE GOD SPEAKS

SCRIPTURE READING

MATTHEW 14:1–12 (NIV)

At that time Herod the tetrarch heard the reports about Jesus, and he said to his attendants, "This is John the Baptist; he has risen from the dead! That is why miraculous powers are at work in him." Now Herod had arrested John and bound him and put him in prison because of Herodias, his brother Philip's wife, for John had been saying to him: "It is not lawful for you to have her." Herod wanted to kill John, but he was afraid of the people, because they considered John a prophet. On Herod's birthday the daughter of Herodias danced for the guests and pleased Herod so much that he promised with an oath to give her whatever she asked. Prompted by her mother, she said, "Give me here on a platter the head of John the Baptist." The king was distressed, but because of his oaths and his dinner guests, he ordered that her request be granted and had John beheaded in the prison. His head was brought in on a platter and given to the girl, who carried it to her mother. John's disciples came and took his body and buried it. Then they went and told Jesus.

SEE ALSO: MARK 6:14–29; LUKE 9:7–9

LIFE LESSONS

This is one of the saddest sections in Scripture. Herod made a flippant remark, one offhand promise while he was probably drunk at a party, and someone else's life ended up on the line. Herod hadn't killed John previously for a reason: to prevent riots among the people—and possibly because Herod recognized there was a chance that John really had been sent by God. But now he was up against a wall. He could either renege on his promise and keep the peace, or he could maintain his pride and murder a prophet of God....

Herod chose to shut down his heart, murdering John the Baptist. Herod feared God, which is why his conscience was troubled by the truth (he knew it was wrong). But he didn't fear God as much as he feared injuring his pride.

Everybody has a conscience. It's that place in your heart where God speaks into your life. Paul stated in Romans 2:15, *"Their own conscience and thoughts either accuse them or tell them they are doing right"* (NLT). Herod initially refused to admit to his sin and imprisoned John the Baptist. Then, he resisted the inner voice of his conscience again and had John killed. His conscience seemed to be just clicking in at the end, when, in his guilt, he stressed that Jesus was John returned to earth.

Don't let pride cloud your conscience. You'll find yourself in a larger mess at the end of it all. Instead, keep looking to God. Keep listening to Him. It's important to admit when we're wrong. Our pride isn't worth hurting ourselves or others.

WHERE ARE YOU?

Have you ever done anything you regretted because of your pride?

_____

_____

_____

_____

Why is it so important to admit when we're wrong?

_____

_____

_____

_____

What wrong have you committed that you might need to acknowledge to God or to others?

_____

_____

_____

_____

A PRAYER

Jesus, keep my heart open to Your message and Your voice. Help me not to let my pride take over my emotions and actions. I pray that I would not be defensive but would always speak the truth. In Your name, amen.

DAY 46:
FOLLOWING OUR SHEPHERD ·

SCRIPTURE READINGS

MATTHEW 14:13–14 (NLT)

As soon as Jesus heard the news, he left in a boat to a remote area to be alone. But the crowds heard where he was headed and followed on foot from many towns. Jesus saw the huge crowd as he stepped from the boat, and he had compassion on them and healed their sick.

MARK 6:30–34 (NLT)

The apostles returned to Jesus from their ministry tour and told him all they had done and taught. Then Jesus said, "Let's go off by ourselves to a quiet place and rest awhile." He said this because there were so many people coming and going that Jesus and his apostles didn't even have time to eat.

So they left by boat for a quiet place, where they could be alone. But many people recognized them and saw them leaving, and people from many towns ran ahead along the shore and got there ahead of them. Jesus saw the huge crowd as he stepped from the boat, and he had compassion on them because they were like sheep without a shepherd. So he began teaching them many things.

SEE ALSO: LUKE 9:10–11; JOHN 6:1–3

LIFE LESSONS

Sheep are mentioned over five hundred times in the Bible. In fact, this animal is mentioned more than any other animal in Scripture. Sheep do not live long without a shepherd. Their flocking instinct directs them to follow a leader, and they are entirely dependent on the shepherd for direction and protection. They require constant guidance and care. If a shepherd were to leave his herd for any amount of time, the sheep would be in great danger.

In this passage, the crowds trail after Jesus as sheep trail after a shepherd. Even when He leaves on a boat to get some space, the people are there when He arrives back on shore. They are *desperately* seeking to follow, to be led, to be cared for. And even though Jesus needs rest, He sees how lost they are. Like a shepherd, Jesus feels that He can't leave them. To do so would be like throwing them back to the wolves.

When we are lost, Jesus has compassion on us. When we show up in front of Him after wandering for a while, He immediately takes us in and continues to embrace us and teach us.

WHERE ARE YOU?

How did Jesus view the crowds of people around Him? And what are some of the things this passage reveals about His character?

How were the people like sheep without a shepherd?

Each day—and especially when you are feeling lost, burdened, or overwhelmed— how can you follow Jesus more closely as your Shepherd?

A PRAYER

Jesus, You are the Great Shepherd. Thank You for protecting me and embracing me after I've wandered and returned. Thank You for Your compassion. I pray that You would guide me through this life. I want to follow You wherever You lead me. In Your name, amen.

DAY 47:
NEVER INSIGNIFICANT

SCRIPTURE READING

JOHN 6:4–13 (CEV)

It was almost time for the Jewish festival of Passover, and Jesus went up on a mountain with his disciples and sat down.

When Jesus saw the large crowd coming toward him, he asked Philip, "Where will we get enough food to feed all these people?" He said this to test Philip, since he already knew what he was going to do.

Philip answered, "Don't you know that it would take almost a year's wages just to buy only a little bread for each of these people?"

Andrew, the brother of Simon Peter, was one of the disciples. He spoke up and said, "There is a boy here who has five small loaves of barley bread and two fish. But what good is that with all these people?"

The ground was covered with grass, and Jesus told his disciples to tell everyone to sit down. About 5,000 men were in the crowd. Jesus took the bread in his hands and gave thanks to God. Then he passed the bread to the people, and he did the same with the fish, until everyone had plenty to eat.

The people ate all they wanted, and Jesus told his disciples to gather up the leftovers, so that nothing would be wasted. The disciples gathered them up and filled twelve large baskets with what was left over from the five barley loaves.

SEE ALSO: MATTHEW 14:15–21; MARK 6:35–44; LUKE 9:12–17

LIFE LESSONS

Aside from the resurrection, the feeding of the five thousand is the only miracle recorded in all four Gospels: Matthew, Mark, Luke, *and* John. It shows that God can take what little we have to give and use it to accomplish incredible things for Him.

While the disciples stood around worrying that there was no way there could possibly be enough food to feed everyone, the boy gave everything he had, and Jesus used it. He broke it, blessed it, and distributed it. The disciples focused only on how great the need was; they fixated on the lack. But they were merely considering earthly options with physical limitations. God wants us to focus on what we do have and on Him. And He can go above and beyond our needs or expectations. Jesus could have provided exactly the amount of fish and bread that the crowd needed. Instead, He provided them with even more than that. They ended up with more leftovers than the amount of food they started with!

Whatever you have, never worry that it's not enough. Whether it is spiritual gifts, talents, time, or resources, God can take it and amplify its impact. Don't focus on the negatives or the lack. Trust in Him and focus on the positives and the possibilities.

WHERE ARE YOU?

In what way was Jesus testing Philip?

_____

_____

_____

_____

_____

What do we learn about Andrew? Why did he even mention the boy's meal if he thought it was inadequate?

_____

_____

_____

_____

_____

Do you ever find yourself focusing on what you don't have rather than on what you do have? What does this passage say about what God can do with us even when we're unsure or feeling inadequate?

_____

_____

_____

_____

_____

A PRAYER

Jesus, thank You for multiplying everything we surrender to You and using it to bless and assist others. Help me to focus on what I am able to give and on the possibilities so that I don't miss the opportunities. Help me to trust fully in Your power. In Your name, amen.

DAY 48:
A TEST OF FAITH

SCRIPTURE READINGS

MATTHEW 14:22–23 (NIV)

Immediately Jesus made the disciples get into the boat and go on ahead of him to the other side, while he dismissed the crowd. After he had dismissed them, he went up on a mountainside by himself to pray. Later that night, he was there alone....

MARK 6:45–46 (MSG)

As soon as the meal was finished, Jesus insisted that the disciples get in the boat and go on ahead across to Bethsaida while he dismissed the congregation. After sending them off, he climbed a mountain to pray.

JOHN 6:14–15 (MSG)

The people realized that God was at work among them in what Jesus had just done. They said, "This is the Prophet for sure, God's Prophet right here in Galilee!" Jesus saw that in their enthusiasm, they were about to grab him and make him king, so he slipped off and went back up the mountain to be by himself.

LIFE LESSONS

Although Jesus put His disciples on a boat and physically left them, that didn't mean He was finished helping them. The situation probably brought great anxiety to His disciples, though. They were separated from Him at a time when they longed to be with Him. But Jesus insisted they travel by themselves on the Sea of Galilee toward Bethsaida, and it's important to note that they went anyway, despite not knowing when they'd see Him again. The disciples weren't privy to the future—they didn't know that they were taking a test of faith.

Tests of faith reveal where we are on our journey with Jesus. Tests also have a way of helping our faith grow stronger. God grows our faith in preparation for what He knows lies ahead. Leaving to go ahead of Jesus was a small test of faith for the disciples to recognize that God was still with them. If it feels like God is sending you on alone, know that He is never far from you.

WHERE ARE YOU?

After doing such an impressive miracle of feeding the five thousand, what is Jesus's response to the situation? What should we probably do, as well, after big life events?

_____

_____

_____

_____

_____

Why is it important to be alone with God after something momentous or stressful occurs?

_____

_____

_____

_____

_____

What tests of your trust in God have you experienced lately?

_____

_____

_____

_____

_____

A PRAYER

Jesus, spiritual tests may be difficult, but I trust that You can use them to grow my faith for whatever my future holds. I pray that my faith would increase over time. Help me to learn all that You are trying to teach me. In Your name, amen.

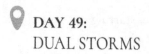

DAY 49:
DUAL STORMS

SCRIPTURE READINGS

MATTHEW 14:24–33 (NLT)

Meanwhile, the disciples were in trouble far away from land, for a strong wind had risen, and they were fighting heavy waves. About three o'clock in the morning Jesus came toward them, walking on the water. When the disciples saw him walking on the water, they were terrified. In their fear, they cried out, "It's a ghost!"

But Jesus spoke to them at once. "Don't be afraid," he said. "Take courage. I am here!" Then Peter called to him, "Lord, if it's really you, tell me to come to you, walking on the water." "Yes, come," Jesus said. So Peter went over the side of the boat and walked on the water toward Jesus. But when he saw the strong wind and the waves, he was terrified and began to sink. "Save me, Lord!" he shouted.

Jesus immediately reached out and grabbed him. "You have so little faith," Jesus said. "Why did you doubt me?" When they climbed back into the boat, the wind stopped. Then the disciples worshiped him. "You really are the Son of God!" they exclaimed.

MARK 6:47–52 (NLT)

Late that night, the disciples were in their boat in the middle of the lake, and Jesus was alone on land. He saw that they were in serious trouble, rowing hard and struggling against the wind and waves. About three o'clock in the morning Jesus came toward them, walking on the water. He intended to go past them, but when they saw him walking on the water, they cried out in terror, thinking he was a ghost. They were all terrified when they saw him.

But Jesus spoke to them at once. "Don't be afraid," he said. "Take courage! I am here!" Then he climbed into the boat, and the wind stopped. They were totally amazed, for they still didn't understand the significance of the miracle of the loaves. Their hearts were too hard to take it in.

SEE ALSO: JOHN 6:16–21

LIFE LESSONS

When we ask God for something, we may be full of confidence and faith, but when it actually comes to pass, our confidence may waver. Asking for big things isn't the same as experiencing them. Likewise, starting out on an endeavor isn't the same as being smack-dab in the middle of it.

In today's Scripture readings, the disciples are facing two storms without Jesus in the boat. The first is a physical storm; the second is a spiritual one due to their lack of faith. For both of these storms, they have to trust Christ over their fear of the surrounding circumstances.

After everything the disciples had done in performing miracles with Jesus's authority, Peter knew that if Jesus empowered him to do so, he could walk on water too. He recognized that the safety of the boat wasn't really that safe. He saw that it is always safer with Jesus. Peter's faith was great enough that he was ready to jump right out onto the water when Jesus said, "Come." But his faith faltered when he looked at the storm swirling all around him.

We will encounter storms in life. There is no way around that reality. There will be rough days even when we're stepping out in faith. We might feel a moment of triumph and then start to sink. If this happens to you, don't let the storm drag you down. Keep your eyes on Jesus. He will not let you sink. He will be there for you.

WHERE ARE YOU?

Why do you think Peter wanted to get out of the boat?

_____

_____

_____

_____

_____

What made him sink?

_____

_____

_____

_____

_____

When have you asked for something and then found it overwhelming later on? How did you handle it? How might you handle such circumstances through trust in God?

_____

_____

_____

_____

_____

A PRAYER

Jesus, help me to have the courage to move out of my comfort zone and into the deeper waters with You. Thank You for catching me when my faith wavers and it feels like I'm drowning. Help me to keep my eyes on You when the storms of life hit. In Your name, amen.

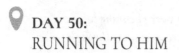

DAY 50:
RUNNING TO HIM

SCRIPTURE READINGS

MATTHEW 14:34–36 (NLT)

After they had crossed the lake, they landed at Gennesaret. When the people recognized Jesus, the news of his arrival spread quickly throughout the whole area, and soon people were bringing all their sick to be healed. They begged him to let the sick touch at least the fringe of his robe, and all who touched him were healed.

MARK 6:53–56 (NLT)

After they had crossed the lake, they landed at Gennesaret. They brought the boat to shore and climbed out. The people recognized Jesus at once, and they ran throughout the whole area, carrying sick people on mats to wherever they heard he was. Wherever he went—in villages, cities, or the countryside—they brought the sick out to the marketplaces. They begged him to let the sick touch at least the fringe of his robe, and all who touched him were healed.

LIFE LESSONS

When Jesus was on earth, people responded to Him in diverse ways: there were groups who wanted Him to leave their presence, groups who reacted to Him in fear, religious leaders who made claims He was a patron of Satan, and others who couldn't get enough of Him.

Today, people respond differently to Jesus as well. Some of us get so busy living our lives that we miss Jesus in the midst of our everyday routines. Some acknowledge Him but never put in any effort to know or follow Him. Some appreciate Jesus as a wonderful teacher but don't accept Him as the Son of God. Many people reject the idea of Jesus entirely. But how many of us energetically seek Him out and run to Him?

During Jesus's ministry, quite a few people followed Him wherever He went. They searched for Him everywhere and longed to be in His presence, even begging to be allowed just to touch the fringe of His robe. From the stories they'd heard, they believed in His healing power.

We all get to choose how we respond to Jesus, how diligently we pursue Him. And if God doesn't seem as close as you want Him to be, that is not on Him.

He reveals Himself to those who seek Him and draw near. It's up to us what we do with our knowledge of Jesus's power and sacrifice for us. Hopefully, it's along the lines of running to Him in gratefulness and love with a hard-driven passion.

WHERE ARE YOU?

What does this passage say about the people and their response to Jesus?

What does it say about Jesus's response to the people?

How will you respond to Jesus today?

A PRAYER

Jesus, I know that my actions are my own, and my decisions are my own. You always want me to seek You more. Help me to draw near to You on a more consistent basis. Give me an unflinching passion for You so I can continue pursuing You, no matter what the circumstances. In Your name, amen.

DAY 51:
WHAT BRINGS YOU HERE?

SCRIPTURE READING

JOHN 6:22–40 (NLT)

The next day the crowd that had stayed on the far shore saw that the disciples had taken the only boat, and they realized Jesus had not gone with them. Several boats from Tiberias landed near the place where the Lord had blessed the bread and the people had eaten. So when the crowd saw that neither Jesus nor his disciples were there, they got into the boats and went across to Capernaum to look for him. They found him on the other side of the lake and asked, "Rabbi, when did you get here?"

Jesus replied, "I tell you the truth, you want to be with me because I fed you, not because you understood the miraculous signs. But don't be so concerned about perishable things like food. Spend your energy seeking the eternal life that the Son of Man can give you. For God the Father has given me the seal of his approval."

They replied, "We want to perform God's works, too. What should we do?"

Jesus told them, "This is the only work God wants from you: Believe in the one he has sent."

They answered, "Show us a miraculous sign if you want us to believe in you. What can you do? After all, our ancestors ate manna while they journeyed through the wilderness! The Scriptures say, 'Moses gave them bread from heaven to eat.'"

Jesus said, "I tell you the truth, Moses didn't give you bread from heaven. My Father did. And now he offers you the true bread from heaven. The true bread of God is the one who comes down from heaven and gives life to the world."

"Sir," they said, "give us that bread every day."

Jesus replied, "I am the bread of life. Whoever comes to me will never be hungry again. Whoever believes in me will never be thirsty. But you haven't believed in me even though you have seen me. However, those the Father has given me will come to me, and I will never reject them. For I have come down from heaven to do the will of God who sent me, not to do my own will. And this is the will of God, that I should not lose even one of all those he has given me, but that I should raise them up at the last day. For it is my Father's will that all who see his Son and believe in him should have eternal life. I will raise them up at the last day."

LIFE LESSONS

What made you want to start following Jesus? What attracted you to His story, to Him? Maybe something just felt right—the words pulled at your heartstrings or made you feel excited, and you weren't sure why. Maybe it all connected for you right away and you understood what Jesus was saying and immediately handed your heart over to Him.

Some of us start out with pure motivations for following Jesus, but others of us take a longer route, winding our way around to committing to Him as we get used to what He's saying. The crowd in this passage followed Him, but not for His teachings, and Jesus called them out on it. He knew His miracle had brought the people, as it was partially meant to do, but now they were staying around for the wrong reasons. They didn't want to listen and change. They weren't inspired to do what it took to be like Him. They wanted to be fed again for free. They wanted to see more miracles. They wanted to be entertained.

Yes, following God comes with blessings, but that doesn't mean our stomachs will always be full, our bank accounts will be flush with cash, or our houses will be located in expensive neighborhoods. The people here showed up where Jesus was because they wanted things for themselves—not to give up things. Although we can ask God for anything, we need to ask ourselves if we're following Him for the right reasons. If we find ourselves primarily hoping for some extra perks or material comforts, we're headed down the wrong road. It's about valuing our relationship with Christ over those things, not about getting all we can.

WHERE ARE YOU?

What did Jesus say was the reason the crowd crossed over to Capernaum to look for Him?

Referring to the time when the Israelites were in the wilderness, where did the people say the "bread from heaven" had come from? Where did Jesus clarify it had actually come from?

_____

_____

_____

_____

We tend to believe only in what we see. But in this passage, what truth did the crowd miss, according to Jesus, even though they saw Him and His miracles, and heard His teaching?

_____

_____

_____

_____

A PRAYER

Jesus, I pray for pure motivations. You provide for me both physically and spiritually, and only You can sustain me forever. Don't let me get caught up in things that will not bring true fulfillment. In Your name, amen.

DAY 52:
PRECONCEIVED NOTIONS

SCRIPTURE READING

JOHN 6:41–59 (NLT)

Then the people began to murmur in disagreement because he had said, "I am the bread that came down from heaven." They said, "Isn't this Jesus, the son of Joseph? We know his father and mother. How can he say, 'I came down from heaven'?"

But Jesus replied, "Stop complaining about what I said. For no one can come to me unless the Father who sent me draws them to me, and at the last day I will raise them up. As it is written in the Scriptures, 'They will all be taught by God.' Everyone who listens to the Father and learns from him comes to me. (Not that anyone has ever seen the Father; only I, who was sent from God, have seen him.)

"I tell you the truth, anyone who believes has eternal life. Yes, I am the bread of life! Your ancestors ate manna in the wilderness, but they all died. Anyone who eats the bread from heaven, however, will never die. I am the living bread that came down from heaven. Anyone who eats this bread will live forever; and this bread, which I will offer so the world may live, is my flesh."

Then the people began arguing with each other about what he meant. "How can this man give us his flesh to eat?" they asked.

So Jesus said again, "I tell you the truth, unless you eat the flesh of the Son of Man and drink his blood, you cannot have eternal life within you. But anyone who eats my flesh and drinks my blood has eternal life, and I will raise that person at the last day. For my flesh is true food, and my blood is true drink. Anyone who eats my flesh and drinks my blood remains in me, and I in him. I live because of the living Father who sent me; in the same way, anyone who feeds on me will live because of me. I am the true bread that came down from heaven. Anyone who eats this bread will not die as your ancestors did (even though they ate the manna) but will live forever."

He said these things while he was teaching in the synagogue in Capernaum.

LIFE LESSONS

We all come into our relationship with Christ carrying some preconceptions. They may be based on our upbringing, previous dealings with the church, stories we've read, or what we've heard other people say. But these preconceptions have a tendency to put Jesus in a box. And He just doesn't fit in boxes.

The people in this story complained because Jesus wasn't what they expected. They knew Jesus as the son of Joseph and Mary, not as the Savior who came down from heaven. When He said He was the *"bread of life,"* they wondered how they were supposed to eat His flesh. Obviously, He didn't mean it in a literal way, but they couldn't see it. They couldn't see past their preconceived notions about what the coming of Christ would look like. You see, Jesus didn't fit their predetermined picture of the promised Messiah of the world. In comparison with whatever they were expecting, Jesus's earthly background and words about being bread from heaven probably seemed pretty ridiculous.

It's essential that we resist putting God in a box. Not everything about Him will make sense to us right away, and even as we learn, we will never be able to fully comprehend Him. Toss away the assumptions you've held that aren't matching up with what you are now learning, keep your mind open, and continue learning. God is far more magnificent than anything we could expect or imagine for ourselves.

WHERE ARE YOU?

Why did the crowd have a difficult time believing Jesus came down from heaven?

_____

_____

_____

_____

_____

Name an incorrect assumption or expectation you had about God or Jesus, either before you became a Christian or early in your walk with Christ. How did your initial perspective change?

_____

_____

_____

_____

Name an inaccurate assumption or expectation you had about being a Christian. How did you resolve that mistaken assumption or expectation?

_____

_____

_____

_____

_____

A PRAYER

Jesus, please forgive me for sometimes trying to put You in a box that I can understand or that fits my expectations. You are too magnificent for my mind to fully comprehend. Help me to leave room for the things about You that I don't yet know or understand. In Your name, amen.

DAY 53:
THERE IS NO HALFWAY

SCRIPTURE READING

JOHN 6:60–65 (NIV)

On hearing it, many of his disciples said, "This is a hard teaching. Who can accept it?"

Aware that his disciples were grumbling about this, Jesus said to them, "Does this offend you? Then what if you see the Son of Man ascend to where he was before! The Spirit gives life; the flesh counts for nothing. The words I have spoken to you—they are full of the Spirit and life. Yet there are some of you who do not believe." For Jesus had known from the beginning which of them did not believe and who would betray him. He went on to say, "This is why I told you that no one can come to me unless the Father has enabled them."

LIFE LESSONS

Jesus used some pretty intense symbolism when He called Himself the "bread of life." This concept is not the easiest to take in when you first hear it, but He was making a distinct point that everyone in attendance completely missed: you have to receive Jesus and His message entirely. This is not a "one foot in, one foot out" kind of deal.

When you eat food and drink water, there is no way to do it halfway. And, with Jesus, there's no halfway or partial commitment either. He didn't come to attract crowds, to have people sit around and just watch Him. He came to make disciples, to change people who would let Him into their lives and allow Him to work on them from the inside out. He was always sifting among the people, finding the truest disciple. He separated those who were willing to listen and act from those who followed Him just for the miracles.

This is the way of Jesus. You have to accept His message in its entirety and commit to Him. There's no doing it halfway.

WHERE ARE YOU?

After hearing Jesus's teaching in the synagogue, what was the complaint of many of His followers?

What has been the hardest thing for you to understand about God? How have you gone about trying to truly comprehend it?

Do you find yourself in a halfway or partial commitment to Jesus today? How will you deal with this condition of your heart?

A PRAYER

Lord, sometimes it can be hard to understand Your words or what You're asking of me, but I pray for the wisdom to get more out of both each day. I want to have complete faith in You and Your ultimate sacrifice for my sins. Help me to be all in. In Your name, amen.

DAY 54:
ACCEPTING "EVEN WHEN..."

SCRIPTURE READING

JOHN 6:66–71 (NIV)

From this time many of his disciples turned back and no longer followed him.

"You do not want to leave too, do you?" Jesus asked the Twelve.

Simon Peter answered him, "Lord, to whom shall we go? You have the words of eternal life. We have come to believe and to know that you are the Holy One of God."

Then Jesus replied, "Have I not chosen you, the Twelve? Yet one of you is a devil!" (He meant Judas, the son of Simon Iscariot, who, though one of the Twelve, was later to betray him.)

LIFE LESSONS

When Jesus asks us to follow Him even when we don't understand, it can feel unnerving. It can make us want to back away a bit. But that's actually a time to *press in* and try to understand, not a time to run away.

Again, some people follow Jesus only for the show or the good feelings. They like being part of something. They like aspects of being involved—like the community or the sense of purpose—but everything about their relationship with God is superficial. When they realize it might cost them something, or when things start going deeper or over their head, they move on to something else, something easier. This is true now, and it was true when Jesus walked the earth. After these particularly difficult teachings, Jesus was left with far fewer followers. The twelve apostles and some others remained with Him—but everyone else deserted Him.

We have to accept Jesus as He is and follow Him even when it doesn't all make sense in our heads yet. Even when we don't understand Him or His teachings, even when it means leaving things, places, and people behind. While salvation is free to the believer, it cost Jesus everything. In return, we give Him true discipleship, which means not bailing when things get confusing or feel less than ideal. If we bow out as soon as it seems more desirable for us to do so, we were probably never all the way in to begin with.

WHERE ARE YOU?

In today's passage, what began happening among Jesus's followers?

_____

_____

_____

_____

When questioned by Jesus, what did Simon Peter declare?

_____

_____

_____

_____

Has there been a time when you thought about backing away from or leaving something but instead continued pressing in and found it was well worth doing so? If so, what happened in that situation?

_____

_____

_____

_____

A PRAYER

Jesus, help me to be consistent in my walk with You—not looking for what's in it for me or getting close to You only when I have something to gain but following You because You are Lord. Help me to accept who You are and what You say, even when it's over my head, even when I'm uncertain. In Your name, amen.

DAY 55:
THE CONDITION OF OUR HEARTS

SCRIPTURE READING

MARK 7:1–13 (msg)

The Pharisees, along with some religion scholars who had come from Jerusalem, gathered around him. They noticed that some of his disciples weren't being careful with ritual washings before meals. The Pharisees—Jews in general, in fact— would never eat a meal without going through the motions of a ritual hand-washing, with an especially vigorous scrubbing if they had just come from the market (to say nothing of the scourings they'd give jugs and pots and pans).

The Pharisees and religion scholars asked, "Why do your disciples brush off the rules, showing up at meals without washing their hands?"

Jesus answered, "Isaiah was right about frauds like you, hit the bull's-eye in fact:

> *These people make a big show of saying the right thing,*
> > *but their heart isn't in it.*
> *They act like they are worshiping me,*
> > *but they don't mean it.*
> *They just use me as a cover*
> > *for teaching whatever suits their fancy,*
> *Ditching God's command*
> > *and taking up the latest fads."*

He went on, "Well, good for you. You get rid of God's command so you won't be inconvenienced in following the religious fashions! Moses said, 'Respect your father and mother,' and, 'Anyone denouncing father or mother should be killed.' But you weasel out of that by saying that it's perfectly acceptable to say to father or mother, 'Gift! What I owed you I've given as a gift to God,' thus relieving yourselves of obligation to father or mother. You scratch out God's Word and scrawl a whim in its place. You do a lot of things like this."

SEE ALSO: MATTHEW 15:1–9

LIFE LESSONS

Has anyone ever questioned your faith because you didn't attend church one Sunday or because you listened to a certain kind of music—or because of any one of the many things they expected a follower of God to do or not do simply because someone decided at some point that one way was holier or "more Christian" than another?

As the Pharisees and religion scholars watched Jesus and His disciples, they noticed that some of the disciples were eating without washing their hands—and that triggered them to take offense. This washing had nothing to do with clean hands. It was a ceremonial washing that stemmed from traditions made by men, not God. Through traditions like these, the Pharisees sought control over others, and they came down hard on Jesus when they noticed He wasn't bending the knee to their rules.

But a relationship with Jesus is not about tradition or what someone decides is the "right way" to live as a Christian. It's about the condition of our hearts. Only you know how it's going between you and God. If someone comes down on you for missing external steps they think you should follow, take it with a grain of salt and turn to God. He is the One who knows what He wants you to do, and He will guide you.

WHERE ARE YOU?

For what reason does Jesus call the Pharisees "frauds" (or "hypocrites," which is the term used in other Bible versions)?

How can we avoid falling into religious hypocrisy or exchanging God's commands for something more "acceptable" to ourselves and others?

If you have ever been chided for not performing certain external religious duties that others expected of you, what were these practices? How did you respond to the criticism?

_____

_____

_____

_____

_____

A PRAYER

Dear God, only You know my heart. I pray that You would examine it and help me to see the motives behind what I do. I pray that I would continue to focus on our relationship, not on what's "expected" of me by others. Help me to seek You when I'm uncertain about what is right. In Jesus's name, amen.

DAY 56:
WHAT COMES FROM INSIDE US

SCRIPTURE READING

MARK 7:14–23 (NLT)

Then Jesus called to the crowd to come and hear. "All of you listen," he said, "and try to understand. It's not what goes into your body that defiles you; you are defiled by what comes from your heart." Then Jesus went into a house to get away from the crowd, and his disciples asked him what he meant by the parable he had just used. "Don't you understand either?" he asked. "Can't you see that the food you put into your body cannot defile you? Food doesn't go into your heart, but only passes through the stomach and then goes into the sewer." (By saying this, he declared that every kind of food is acceptable in God's eyes.) And then he added, "It is what comes from inside that defiles you. For from within, out of a person's heart, come evil thoughts, sexual immorality, theft, murder, adultery, greed, wickedness, deceit, lustful desires, envy, slander, pride, and foolishness. All these vile things come from within; they are what defile you."

SEE ALSO: MATTHEW 15:10–20

LIFE LESSONS

How do you know if you're really investing in your relationship with Jesus so that He can do His work in You? Take a good hard look at what's coming out of your heart. Consider your recent thoughts, words, and actions. How did you speak to that friend when you were angry? What did you choose to do when you were caught in a lie? What have you been saying about your coworker behind their back when you're nice to them in person? Your words and actions will help you determine what's already deep down in your heart.

The religious leaders of Jesus's day had it all wrong. Corruption doesn't enter your life from the outside and work its way in. Defilement starts on the inside of your heart and works its way out. Listening to an inappropriate song isn't going to immediately filthy up our soul, although it's not what we should be taking in regularly. Jesus tells us where sin originates, and it's not with what we take in. Sin is an inside job.

Our thoughts, our attitudes, our true nature in our hearts are what overflow into the words and actions that permeate our lives. The only way to be "clean" or pure is to start working on things from the inside and allowing Jesus to transform us.

WHERE ARE YOU?

What is Jesus's explanation of what defiles us as believers?

_____

_____

_____

_____

_____

When have you been surprised by a negative reaction that just seemed to "come right out" of you? What is the best way to respond when that happens?

_____

_____

_____

_____

_____

Why is it still important to be careful about what we allow into our lives—what we dwell on, see, and hear?

_____

_____

_____

_____

_____

A PRAYER

Jesus, I pray that You would work in me. I want my words and actions to be reminiscent of Yours. I want to focus on what's important: cleaning up from the inside out. Help me to stay focused on the right things. In Your name, amen.

DAY 57:
EVERYONE BELONGS

SCRIPTURE READING

MARK 7:24–30 (NLT)

Then Jesus left Galilee and went north to the region of Tyre. He didn't want anyone to know which house he was staying in, but he couldn't keep it a secret. Right away a woman who had heard about him came and fell at his feet. Her little girl was possessed by an evil spirit, and she begged him to cast out the demon from her daughter.

Since she was a Gentile, born in Syrian Phoenicia, Jesus told her, "First I should feed the children—my own family, the Jews. It isn't right to take food from the children and throw it to the dogs."

She replied, "That's true, Lord, but even the dogs under the table are allowed to eat the scraps from the children's plates."

"Good answer!" he said. "Now go home, for the demon has left your daughter." And when she arrived home, she found her little girl lying quietly in bed, and the demon was gone.

SEE ALSO: MATTHEW 15:21–28

LIFE LESSONS

In this passage, it looks at first as if Jesus is going to dismiss the woman, but instead He makes one thing very clear: He came for everyone—something that not even the disciples anticipated (they expected a Messiah for the Jews alone). Jesus came for Jews *and* their enemies alike.

If you ever feel like you aren't worthy or that God shouldn't waste His time on you, toss those thoughts out the window right now! None of us has earned God's favor, and the whole point is that we couldn't if we tried. Jesus did for us what we could not do for ourselves, securing our salvation and a restored relationship with the Father through His sacrifice on the cross. He came for all of us, regardless of our ancestry, race, family background, societal status, health issues, or anything else.

There are so many things we don't get to choose about ourselves, but that's no reason to ever feel like we don't belong. Everyone belongs in the kingdom of God.

The woman knew it could be asking a lot for Jesus to save her Gentile daughter, but she came to Him anyway. She came *"right away."* Anyone who accepts

Jesus belongs. All who humble themselves will see the work of Jesus. He calls to every heart.

WHERE ARE YOU?

When the woman approached Jesus, whom did He say He was there to help?

_____
_____
_____
_____

What did the woman say to Jesus that saved her daughter?

_____
_____
_____
_____

When you feel like you don't deserve something, do you approach God and ask for it anyway? Why or why not?

_____
_____
_____
_____

A PRAYER

Jesus, help me to feel confident in Your love for me. You came for everyone. Help me not to look down on myself. Heal the parts of my heart that are still broken from past hurts, and enable me to give You my whole heart. In Your name, amen.

DAY 58:
ONE-ON-ONE WITH JESUS

SCRIPTURE READING

MARK 7:31–37 (NLT)

Jesus left Tyre and went up to Sidon before going back to the Sea of Galilee and the region of the Ten Towns. A deaf man with a speech impediment was brought to him, and the people begged Jesus to lay his hands on the man to heal him.

Jesus led him away from the crowd so they could be alone. He put his fingers into the man's ears. Then, spitting on his own fingers, he touched the man's tongue. Looking up to heaven, he sighed and said, "Ephphatha," which means, "Be opened!" Instantly the man could hear perfectly, and his tongue was freed so he could speak plainly!

Jesus told the crowd not to tell anyone, but the more he told them not to, the more they spread the news. They were completely amazed and said again and again, "Everything he does is wonderful. He even makes the deaf to hear and gives speech to those who cannot speak."

LIFE LESSONS

Not every miracle is meant to be a spectacle to cause everyone to believe. Some miracles are intimate, between us and God. The way He works in each of us is unique because it's about relationship and not just God making our lives better. He wants us to listen to Him, to comprehend what He's doing, and to appreciate it but also learn from it.

Notice how gentle Jesus is with this man. He takes him away from the crowd, and instead of just speaking to the deaf man, He uses His fingers to indicate what's coming, demonstrating in a way the man can understand that He's working on his ears and mouth.

When we need it, Jesus will be just as gentle with us. For us to experience this, though, we might need to let Him pull us away from the crowd so He can work with us one-on-one.

WHERE ARE YOU?

In today's Scripture, what act did Jesus perform in the healing of the man that was more personal than any we have read so far?

_____

_____

_____

_____

_____

Do you believe Jesus really thought the crowd would not go out and spread the word about the miracle they had witnessed?

_____

_____

_____

_____

_____

How has God worked in your heart in your time alone with Him?

_____

_____

_____

_____

_____

A PRAYER

Jesus, thank You for caring for me. Thank You for Your gentle nature and Your desire to heal us. Help me to set aside time with You one-on-one so You can work in my life and heal what needs to be healed. In Your name, amen.

DAY 59:
LAYING IT ALL DOWN

SCRIPTURE READING

MATTHEW 15:29–31 (NLT)

Jesus returned to the Sea of Galilee and climbed a hill and sat down. A vast crowd brought to him people who were lame, blind, crippled, those who couldn't speak, and many others. They laid them before Jesus, and he healed them all. The crowd was amazed! Those who hadn't been able to speak were talking, the crippled were made well, the lame were walking, and the blind could see again! And they praised the God of Israel.

LIFE LESSONS

What a sight that must have been—crowds bringing an endless line of people to be healed and laying them before Jesus. Just imagine all the mute people suddenly talking, all the crippled people walking, and all the blind people seeing. With everything that was happening, the people couldn't help but be amazed. It makes sense that they responded in the way they did, by praising the God who heals. It would have been hard not to. They might not have been sure who Jesus was, but they had faith in His healing power, and they were in awe of it.

God does similar miracles in our lives today in the spiritual realm. We lay our brokenness before Him, our hurts and our pains, and He heals them. When we're weak, He strengthens us. When we're sad, He wipes away our tears. There is so much we can lay before Him. There is so much we can ask of Him with confidence. He loves giving His children good gifts.

WHERE ARE YOU?

Once the people were healed, whom did the crowd praise, and why?

What burdens or problems have you laid before Jesus lately, seeking His strength and healing? What might you lay before Him right now?

_____

_____

_____

_____

_____

What type of healing have you seen God do in someone else's life lately? How might you offer Him praise for it today?

_____

_____

_____

_____

_____

A PRAYER

God, You are the great Healer. Thank You for healing so many parts of my life. Thank You for letting me lay all my concerns before You. Help me to have the same confidence in Your power to heal that the crowd at the Sea of Galilee had. Help me to always keep the same sense of awe at what You are capable of doing. In Jesus's name, amen.

DAY 60:
THE GOOD SHEPHERD FEEDS HIS SHEEP

SCRIPTURE READING

MARK 8:1–10 (CEV)

One day another large crowd gathered around Jesus. They had not brought along anything to eat. So Jesus called his disciples together and said, "I feel sorry for these people. They have been with me for three days, and they don't have anything to eat. Some of them live a long way from here. If I send them away hungry, they might faint on their way home."

The disciples said, "This place is like a desert. Where can we find enough food to feed such a crowd?"

Jesus asked them how much food they had. They replied, "Seven small loaves of bread."

After Jesus told the crowd to sit down, he took the seven loaves and gave thanks. He then broke the loaves and handed them to his disciples, who passed them out to the crowd. They also had a few little fish, and after Jesus had blessed these, he told the disciples to pass them around.

The crowd of about 4,000 people ate all they wanted, and the leftovers filled seven large baskets.

As soon as Jesus had sent the people away, he got into the boat with the disciples and crossed to the territory near Dalmanutha.

SEE ALSO: MATTHEW 15:32–39

LIFE LESSONS

Once again, when faced with a need, the disciples reacted with uncertainty. Once again, all they saw was a lack of resources. But Jesus was ready. He is always ready. When all we see is what we lack, when all we feel is empty, He is there, ready to fill us and to transform what may seem insignificant into something great.

There are some common threads here that we've seen before. Some scholars have noted that Jesus concluded each segment of His ministry with feeding events. He finished His ministry in Galilee with the feeding of the five thousand, and He completed His ministry in the region of the Gentiles with the feeding of the four thousand. Then, He ended His Judean ministry by feeding His disciples in the upper room. And He's made the point multiple times that while physical food is temporary, what He gives fills us forever.

The Good Shepherd feeds His sheep. He takes care of us. Jesus wants to nourish us. He wants to make sure we're spiritually full. He doesn't just bring us partway. He doesn't welcome us in and then leave us on our own—hungry, faint, and weak—to figure it out for ourselves. He teaches us, refills us when we need it, and sends us out.

Trust that He'll be there to provide for you. And not just the bare minimum. He wants your heart to overflow. For your soul to be satisfied.

WHERE ARE YOU?

What do you believe is the significance of the leftovers indicated in the gospel accounts of Matthew and Mark of Jesus feeding the multitudes?

_____

_____

_____

_____

_____

When has God given you more than you expected?

_____

_____

_____

_____

_____

Describe in your own words what you think it means to be spiritually "fed" by Jesus.

A PRAYER

Jesus, I know that You will fill my heart, giving me renewed energy, renewed hope, and a renewed spirit when I seek You. You are the only One who can satisfy my soul. Help me to trust in You to provide when I'm struggling and feel like I'm going on empty. In Your name, amen.

DAY 61:
TAKING A SECOND LOOK

SCRIPTURE READINGS

MATTHEW 16:1–4 (NLT)

One day the Pharisees and Sadducees came to test Jesus, demanding that he show them a miraculous sign from heaven to prove his authority.

He replied, "You know the saying, 'Red sky at night means fair weather tomorrow; red sky in the morning means foul weather all day.' You know how to interpret the weather signs in the sky, but you don't know how to interpret the signs of the times! Only an evil, adulterous generation would demand a miraculous sign, but the only sign I will give them is the sign of the prophet Jonah." Then Jesus left them and went away.

MARK 8:11–13 (NLT)

When the Pharisees heard that Jesus had arrived, they came and started to argue with him. Testing him, they demanded that he show them a miraculous sign from heaven to prove his authority.

When he heard this, he sighed deeply in his spirit and said, "Why do these people keep demanding a miraculous sign? I tell you the truth, I will not give this generation any such sign." So he got back into the boat and left them, and he crossed to the other side of the lake.

LIFE LESSONS

It's hard not to feel exasperated when we read about these demands from the religious leaders. By this point in time, Jesus had already given signs. He had done His works right in front of their noses, and they knew it. Yet, even though they had witnessed His power and authority time and time again, they still asked for *another* sign.

It was the religious crowd that frustrated Jesus the most. He didn't need their personal validation to be who He already was. He was the Messiah, whether they accepted that reality or not. They chose to disregard the signs that were already there. They ignored common sense as they tried to take the situation into their own hands and influence it.

We humans can be so blind to truth that goes against what we want or hope for. We do everything we can to ignore that truth or to mold our situations into something over which we have more control. We might even become angry with God or try to test Him. As a result, we miss everything He is trying to show us—the truth that's right under our noses. The signs can be all around us, but when we're in this state of denial, we don't notice or acknowledge them. This is why it's so important to let go of our desire to control everything, take a step back, open our hearts and minds, and, with fresh eyes, take a second look at what God is saying and doing.

WHERE ARE YOU?

What do you think Jesus is saying about signs in this passage?

When have you ignored something real just because you didn't want it to be true? What happened when you finally acknowledged that it was true anyway?

Have you been resisting or ignoring any truths God has been showing you? If so, how can you change your response to Him today?

A PRAYER

Jesus, I'm sorry that I sometimes ignore what You are doing because it's not what I thought or hoped it would be. I know You are present all around me and are always revealing Yourself in various ways. I pray that You would open my eyes to Your presence so I can appreciate what You *are* doing in my life, all the time. In Your name, amen.

DAY 62:
HE WILL COME THROUGH FOR YOU

SCRIPTURE READING

MARK 8:14–21 (CEV)

The disciples had forgotten to bring any bread, and they had only one loaf with them in the boat. Jesus warned them, "Watch out! Guard against the yeast of the Pharisees and of Herod."

The disciples talked this over and said to each other, "He must be saying this because we don't have any bread."

Jesus knew what they were thinking and asked, "Why are you talking about not having any bread? Don't you understand? Are your minds still closed? Are your eyes blind and your ears deaf? Don't you remember how many baskets of leftovers you picked up when I fed those 5,000 people with only five small loaves of bread?"

"Yes," the disciples answered. "There were twelve baskets."

Jesus then asked, "And how many baskets of leftovers did you pick up when I broke seven small loaves of bread for those 4,000 people?"

"Seven," they answered.

"Don't you know what I am talking about by now?" Jesus asked.

SEE ALSO: MATTHEW 16:5–12

LIFE LESSONS

We often worry when we hit rough patches in life, even if we have experienced God come through for us hundreds of times. He has carried us and provided for us, yet somehow we forget about those times. Again and again.

Jesus had miraculously fed five thousand people and then four thousand, but in this passage, the disciples were sitting in the boat, arguing about their single loaf of bread and how it wasn't sufficient to feed everyone present. (Bear in mind, there was a total of only thirteen people this time, not thousands, to be fed.) It's enough to make your jaw drop. They had watched Jesus take care of multitudes when He had begun with so little, but it still didn't cross their minds to ask for and trust in His help!

The disciples immediately turned to worry, not to Jesus. Even after all they'd experienced, they weren't sure that He would provide what was needed and take care of them. They wanted food (which, of course, we all need), but what they really needed was to trust Jesus first—and remember what they'd already seen Him do with their own eyes. They were acting just like the religious leaders, always needing one more miracle to really believe in what Jesus was doing, while overlooking what was happening right in front of them.

It's important to trust Jesus first and to remember what He's done for us in the past. He's come through for us before—and He will do so again.

WHERE ARE YOU?

How does this passage show us that Jesus gives us what we need to believe in Him?

_____

_____

_____

_____

_____

Jesus encourages the disciples to remember past miracles in order to have faith for miracles in the moment. Record (either in writing or through an audio or video recording) a time when God has been faithful to you.

_____

_____

_____

_____

_____

How can remembering God's faithfulness in the past help you to remain faithful to Him in the present?

_____

_____

_____

_____

A PRAYER

Jesus, I know my faith is lacking even though You've done countless miracles and have always been there for me. Don't let me overlook You on the hard days. Give me faith to trust You more. Thank You for providing for me in times of need. In Your name, amen.

DAY 63:
A PERFECT PART OF GOD'S PLAN

SCRIPTURE READING

MARK 8:22–26 (MSG)

They arrived at Bethsaida. Some people brought a sightless man and begged Jesus to give him a healing touch. Taking him by the hand, he led him out of the village. He put spit in the man's eyes, laid hands on him, and asked, "Do you see anything?"

He looked up. "I see men. They look like walking trees." So Jesus laid hands on his eyes again. The man looked hard and realized that he had recovered perfect sight, saw everything in bright, twenty-twenty focus. Jesus sent him straight home, telling him, "Don't enter the village."

LIFE LESSONS

Jesus does all things perfectly—He does them fully and appropriately, with intention. He could have healed this man instantly, but He chose to heal him gradually, in two stages.

This progressive miracle, in contrast to an immediate miracle, is similar to the gradual spiritual growth of Jesus's disciples. As they continued to follow Jesus, their spiritual eyes were opened wider. This progression gave them time to fully process everything, to understand the nuances and meaning behind what Jesus was saying and doing, and to learn Jesus's character. It was all leading to a fuller revelation of Him. Their faith wouldn't have been the same otherwise.

Similarly, as we begin to follow Jesus, God starts to open our spiritual eyes. Slowly, over the years, He reveals more of Himself and His ways, and we grow and mature in our Christian walk. So, don't worry about rushing things. The process is a perfect part of God's plan.

WHERE ARE YOU?

Why do you think Jesus leads the man out of the village to heal him?

_____

_____

_____

_____

What are the benefits of learning things gradually or getting to know someone over time?

_____

_____

_____

_____

_____

What are some ways God has opened your spiritual eyes?

_____

_____

_____

_____

_____

A PRAYER

Jesus, thank You for walking with me daily through this journey of life. I know I need Your gentle reminders that developing maturity takes time. Give me patience as I work through the challenges of each day. Help me to release my frustration to You when I wish I were farther along in my spiritual walk than I am and to trust in Your faithfulness to transform me into Your likeness. In Your name, amen.

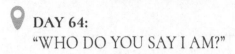

DAY 64:
"WHO DO YOU SAY I AM?"

SCRIPTURE READING

MATTHEW 16:13–20 (CEV)

When Jesus and his disciples were near the town of Caesarea Philippi, he asked them, "What do people say about the Son of Man?"

The disciples answered, "Some people say you are John the Baptist or maybe Elijah or Jeremiah or some other prophet."

Then Jesus asked, "But who do you say I am?"

Simon Peter spoke up, "You are the Messiah, the Son of the living God."

Jesus told him:

"Simon, son of Jonah, you are blessed! You didn't discover this on your own. It was shown to you by my Father in heaven. So I will call you Peter, which means 'a rock.' On this rock I will build my church, and death itself will not have any power over it. I will give you the keys to the kingdom of heaven, and God in heaven will allow whatever you allow on earth. But he will not allow anything you don't allow."

Jesus told his disciples not to tell anyone he was the Messiah.

SEE ALSO: MARK 8:27–30; LUKE 9:18–22

LIFE LESSONS

Our impressions of the world and other people change over time, but there are some absolutes that never change, even if our understanding about them does. One of those absolutes is who Jesus is. People around the world may call Him by different names, everyone might experience Him in a different way, and people might have some different interpretations of His words—but regardless of how we were introduced to Him, how we interact with Him, or where we are in our relationship with Him, Jesus is still the Son of God.

Do we believe that? Is Jesus really God to us? Have we truly recognized Him for who He is?

This is the one unavoidable question that everyone who has ever been introduced to Jesus faces: "Who is He?" People throughout history have debated the answer. This question has divided nations and families. But the real question ends up being, "Who is He to *you*?" It's not about who other people decide He is. It's about who you believe Him to be.

When Jesus asked His disciples, in effect, "Who do people say I am?" their answers were all over the place. Then, when Jesus personalized the question to ask, *"But who do you say I am?"* Peter answered from his personal experience, from what he knew to be true based on the time he'd spent with Jesus—living alongside Him, listening to His teachings, and watching Him perform miracles.

This is a question you can only really answer by spending time in a relationship with Jesus. Knowing Him personally is so important, and no one else can do that for you. You have to know in your *own* heart who He is.

WHERE ARE YOU?

Jesus asked His disciples, "Who do people say that I am?" How would you answer that question today?

_____

_____

_____

_____

_____

Jesus continues to ask His followers, "Who do you say that I am?" How would you answer this question?

_____

_____

_____

_____

_____

Why do you think Jesus instructed His disciples not to tell anyone He was the Messiah?

_____

_____

_____

_____

_____

A PRAYER

Lord Jesus, thank You for being a personal Savior. Help me to know—really *know* deep in my heart—that You are the Son of God who came to save us. Please speak to me and help me to listen and to understand clearly what You are saying. In Your name, amen.

DAY 65:
THE RIGHT PERSPECTIVE CAN CHANGE EVERYTHING

SCRIPTURE READINGS

MATTHEW 16:21–23 (CEV)

From then on, Jesus began telling his disciples what would happen to him. He said, "I must go to Jerusalem. There the nation's leaders, the chief priests, and the teachers of the Law of Moses will make me suffer terribly. I will be killed, but three days later I will rise to life."

Peter took Jesus aside and told him to stop talking like that. He said, "God would never let this happen to you, Lord!"

Jesus turned to Peter and said, "Satan, get away from me! You're in my way because you think like everyone else and not like God."

MARK 8:31–33 (NIV)

He then began to teach them that the Son of Man must suffer many things and be rejected by the elders, the chief priests and the teachers of the law, and that he must be killed and after three days rise again. He spoke plainly about this, and Peter took him aside and began to rebuke him.

But when Jesus turned and looked at his disciples, he rebuked Peter. "Get behind me, Satan!" he said. "You do not have in mind the concerns of God, but merely human concerns."

LIFE LESSONS

Peter couldn't imagine the scenario Jesus was describing actually happening. It didn't fit with how he saw the coming of the Messiah or even how he saw Jesus based on the time he had spent with Him. What Jesus was saying sounded ridiculous and frightening to Peter. But it was all for a greater purpose.

Jesus's perception of what was to come is explained in Hebrews 12:2: *"Because of the joy awaiting him, he endured the cross, disregarding its shame"* (NLT). Jesus was able to endure the cross because He envisioned the results God had revealed to Him. He saw His Father's will and purpose, which enabled Him to complete His Father's plan.

A proper perspective can change everything, and seeing things from God's perspective takes practice. The only way to gain greater insight into His will and perspective is to spend time with Him, read His Word with an open heart, and pray for His discernment.

WHERE ARE YOU?

When Jesus foretold the manner of His death, why do you think the disciples had a hard time believing it would happen that way?

_____

_____

_____

_____

_____

When has a change in your perspective made a huge difference in your life, such as how you approached something?

_____

_____

_____

_____

_____

Think of a time when you realized you didn't have in mind God's concerns about something but only human concerns. How did you respond to that realization? How can you better align yourself with God's perspective and purposes?

_____

_____

_____

_____

_____

A PRAYER

Jesus, when I can't see the long-term goals or paths in Your purposes, what's happening around me can seem absurd or scary. But You always have a plan. Help me to draw closer to You so that Your purpose and perspective can be clearer to me. In Your name, amen.

DAY 66:
GREATER THAN ANYTHING IN THIS WORLD

SCRIPTURE READINGS

MATTHEW 16:24–28 (CEV)

Then Jesus said to his disciples:

If any of you want to be my followers, you must forget about yourself. You must take up your cross and follow me. If you want to save your life, you will destroy it. But if you give up your life for me, you will find it. What will you gain, if you own the whole world but destroy yourself? What would you give to get back your soul?

The Son of Man will soon come in the glory of his Father and with his angels to reward all people for what they have done. I promise you some of those standing here will not die before they see the Son of Man coming with his kingdom.

LUKE 9:23–27 (NLT)

Then he said to the crowd, "If any of you wants to be my follower, you must give up your own way, take up your cross daily, and follow me. If you try to hang on to your life, you will lose it. But if you give up your life for my sake, you will save it. And what do you benefit if you gain the whole world but are yourself lost or destroyed? If anyone is ashamed of me and my message, the Son of Man will be ashamed of that person when he returns in his glory and in the glory of the Father and the holy angels. I tell you the truth, some standing here right now will not die before they see the Kingdom of God."

SEE ALSO: MARK 8:34–38; 9:1

LIFE LESSONS

Human beings generally like hanging on to things—we like our comforts, our beliefs and opinions, our routines, and our successes. We have a hard time letting these things go, and we feel pressured to maintain them, convinced by others that some of these things are as good as life gets. But Jesus says we can't have the things of this world *and* follow Him—not if He asks us to let something go.

Nowhere does Scripture teach that the Christian life is easy! Jesus compares it to taking up your own cross. That's not a pleasant comparison. But He also assures us that those who do so, who follow Him, will find it more than worth it. Following Him is about letting go of our own plans, our own selfish desires and whims. We have to give up doing things our own way.

When we hold on to the world too tightly, we can't fully let God in. We lose sight of the spiritual significance of eternity and God's plan for us. That's why we have to let go of who we thought we were and what we thought we wanted for ourselves and let Him show us who we are and what He wants for us. We can't have it both ways, and God's reward is much greater than anything we will find in this life.

WHERE ARE YOU?

What do you think Jesus means by this statement from Luke 9:24 (NLT): "If you try to hang on to your life, you will lose it. But if you give up your life for my sake, you will save it"?

What do you have the hardest time surrendering to God—something you know He is asking you to give up, stop doing, or change?

What can you do to intentionally "give up your own way" as described in Luke 9:23 (NLT)?

_____

_____

_____

_____

_____

A PRAYER

Jesus, I realize that I sometimes seek after worldly things more than I follow after Your will for my life. Help me to understand that nothing is more important than surrendering my life to You. Help me to loosen my grip on this world so I can focus on what is most important. In Your name, amen.

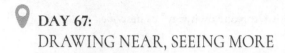

DAY 67:
DRAWING NEAR, SEEING MORE

SCRIPTURE READING

MARK 9:2–13 (MSG)

*Six days later, three of them did see it ["the kingdom of God arrive in full force,"
Mark 9:1 MSG]. Jesus took Peter, James, and John and led them up a high mountain. His appearance changed from the inside out, right before their eyes. His
clothes shimmered, glistening white, whiter than any bleach could make them.
Elijah, along with Moses, came into view, in deep conversation with Jesus.*

*Peter interrupted, "Rabbi, this is a great moment! Let's build three memorials—
one for you, one for Moses, one for Elijah." He blurted this out without thinking,
stunned as they all were by what they were seeing.*

*Just then a light-radiant cloud enveloped them, and from deep in the cloud, a
voice: "This is my Son, marked by my love. Listen to him."*

*The next minute the disciples were looking around, rubbing their eyes, seeing
nothing but Jesus, only Jesus.*

*Coming down the mountain, Jesus swore them to secrecy. "Don't tell a soul what
you saw. After the Son of Man rises from the dead, you're free to talk." They puzzled over that, wondering what on earth "rising from the dead" meant.*

*Meanwhile they were asking, "Why do the religion scholars say that Elijah has to
come first?"*

*Jesus replied, "Elijah does come first and get everything ready for the coming of
the Son of Man. They treated this Elijah like dirt, much like they will treat the
Son of Man, who will, according to Scripture, suffer terribly and be kicked around
contemptibly."*

SEE ALSO: MATTHEW 17:1–13; LUKE 9:28–36

LIFE LESSONS

On three different occasions, Jesus took three specific disciples—Peter, James,
and John—into a deeper encounter with Him. The three encounters were
Jesus raising Jairus's daughter from the dead (see, for example, Luke 8:40–
42, 49–56), Jesus praying in the garden of Gethsemane (see, for example,

Matthew 26:36–45), and Jesus's transfiguration, as described in Mark 9:2, as well as other gospels. Now Jesus had twelve disciples. Why did He take just these three to witness these special occasions?

There isn't an easy answer to that question, but what we do know is that these three men became prominent leaders in the early church. It's not that Jesus loves some of His children more—it's just that some are closer to Him than others. And those who are closer to Him will see more of His glory and more of His power than those who stay farther away. Think about it. We are as close to God as we desire to be. These disciples drew close, and more was revealed to them in advance. The more we draw near and the closer we are to God, the more we will see of Him. This is something that you have some control over! Will you choose to draw nearer to God today?

WHERE ARE YOU?

What do you think is the significance of Jesus's transformation in appearance and His clothing becoming "glistening[ly] white"?

_____

_____

_____

_____

_____

Have there been times when you have had a greater sense of Jesus's glory (perhaps while reading God's Word or worshipping Him)? If so, how did you respond?

_____

_____

_____

_____

_____

How might you draw closer to God today?

_____

_____

_____

_____

_____

A PRAYER

Jesus, I want to see more of You in my life. Help me to spend more time in Your presence, continually seeking You. Draw me closer and closer to You. In Your name, amen.

DAY 68:
RELIANT FOR LIFE

SCRIPTURE READING

MARK 9:14–29 (NLT)

When they returned to the other disciples, they saw a large crowd surrounding them, and some teachers of religious law were arguing with them. When the crowd saw Jesus, they were overwhelmed with awe, and they ran to greet him. "What is all this arguing about?" Jesus asked. One of the men in the crowd spoke up and said, "Teacher, I brought my son so you could heal him. He is possessed by an evil spirit that won't let him talk. And whenever this spirit seizes him, it throws him violently to the ground. Then he foams at the mouth and grinds his teeth and becomes rigid. So I asked your disciples to cast out the evil spirit, but they couldn't do it."

Jesus said to them, "You faithless people! How long must I be with you? How long must I put up with you? Bring the boy to me." So they brought the boy. But when the evil spirit saw Jesus, it threw the child into a violent convulsion, and he fell to the ground, writhing and foaming at the mouth. "How long has this been happening?" Jesus asked the boy's father. He replied, "Since he was a little boy. The spirit often throws him into the fire or into water, trying to kill him. Have mercy on us and help us, if you can."

"What do you mean, 'If I can'?" Jesus asked. "Anything is possible if a person believes." The father instantly cried out, "I do believe, but help me overcome my unbelief!"

When Jesus saw that the crowd of onlookers was growing, he rebuked the evil spirit. "Listen, you spirit that makes this boy unable to hear and speak," he said. "I command you to come out of this child and never enter him again!"

Then the spirit screamed and threw the boy into another violent convulsion and left him. The boy appeared to be dead. A murmur ran through the crowd as people said, "He's dead." But Jesus took him by the hand and helped him to his feet, and he stood up. Afterward, when Jesus was alone in the house with his disciples, they asked him, "Why couldn't we cast out that evil spirit?" Jesus replied, "This kind can be cast out only by prayer."

SEE ALSO: MATTHEW 17:14–21; LUKE 9:37–42

LIFE LESSONS

God doesn't send us off to do our own thing, relying on our own powers and abilities. Although He empowers us, we have to remember that we are still reliant on Him—*always*. That reality doesn't change, regardless of how long we've been walking with Jesus or how much we've done through Him.

Sometimes, in the early days of knowing God, our faith is more open to Him, more welcoming of His help. And God responds to this! He often does more with a person who has newfound faith than He does with someone who has been a longtime believer but has started believing *they* are doing the work rather than God. No matter where you are in your journey with Jesus, it's always about Him—believing in Him and what *He* can do. It's not about us.

The disciples were pretty confused when they couldn't help this father and son. They kept trying to do it themselves, and they became frustrated. When you become frustrated because it seems like something you want to do for God isn't working, it's probably time to pray, because faith isn't about doing what we want. Faith is about doing what God wants.

Anything is possible for someone who truly believes. And in the spirit of this devoted father, it's always good to reach out to God when we sense our faith dwindling. When believing feels like too much, too impossible, just ask God for help.

WHERE ARE YOU?

The disciples in this story who lacked faith had been away from Jesus. What do you think proximity to Jesus has to do with the strength of our faith?

In what situation do you feel the need to pray the prayer of the father in this story: "I do believe, but help me overcome my unbelief!"?

_____
_____
_____
_____
_____

What issue in your life needs consistent prayer these days?

_____
_____
_____
_____
_____

A PRAYER

Jesus, I have faith in You, but some areas of my faith are still weak. Help me to overcome my unbelief. I am powerless by myself. It's all You. Help me to rely on You fully, and strengthen my faith in You. In Your name, amen.

DAY 69:
THERE'S MORE TO COME

SCRIPTURE READINGS

MATTHEW 17:22–23 (NLT)

After they gathered again in Galilee, Jesus told them, "The Son of Man is going to be betrayed into the hands of his enemies. He will be killed, but on the third day he will be raised from the dead." And the disciples were filled with grief.

MARK 9:30–32 (NLT)

Leaving that region, they traveled through Galilee. Jesus didn't want anyone to know he was there, for he wanted to spend more time with his disciples and teach them. He said to them, "The Son of Man is going to be betrayed into the hands of his enemies. He will be killed, but three days later he will rise from the dead." They didn't understand what he was saying, however, and they were afraid to ask him what he meant.

LUKE 9:43–45 (NLT)

Awe gripped the people as they saw this majestic display of God's power.

While everyone was marveling at everything he was doing, Jesus said to his disciples, "Listen to me and remember what I say. The Son of Man is going to be betrayed into the hands of his enemies." But they didn't know what he meant. Its significance was hidden from them, so they couldn't understand it, and they were afraid to ask him about it.

LIFE LESSONS

Nobody likes to think or talk about death. We can't wrap our heads around it. From a worldly point of view, the subject of death is sad and gloomy, but from a spiritual point of view, death can be glorious, not something to fear. From this side, death seems like the end, but from heaven's side, it is only the beginning.

When Jesus predicted His death *again* to His disciples, it must have been difficult to hear. Repeatedly, Jesus had told them He was going to die. But He didn't mean for this to be a reason for grief. Jesus knew that what came afterward would be remarkable, a reason for celebration. It makes you wonder if the disciples missed the part about His rising from the dead or if they just plain skipped over it because it sounded impossible. Were they so focused on His words about death that they missed His words about rising again, about deliverance?

The unknown can be terrifying, to be sure. If you're afraid of death, you are not alone in that. But God can help us change our perspective. There is more to come. There is eternity waiting for us. Rather than seeing death as an exit, we can start viewing it as a step into eternity, into forever with God.

WHERE ARE YOU?

Why did Jesus tell His disciples about His approaching death and resurrection?

How does your view of death shape the way you live life?

How can you gain a heavenly perspective in your attitude toward death?

A PRAYER

Jesus, I praise You that this life is not the only one we get to live. Thank You for having something even better waiting for us in eternity with You. Help me to see death through Your eyes, Your perspective, not mine. Thank You for "setting eternity in our hearts," as it says in Ecclesiastes 3:11 (NIV). In Your name, amen.

DAY 70:
GRACIOUS TOWARD AUTHORITY

SCRIPTURE READING

MATTHEW 17:24–27 (NIV)

After Jesus and his disciples arrived in Capernaum, the collectors of the two-drachma temple tax came to Peter and asked, "Doesn't your teacher pay the temple tax?"

"Yes, he does," he replied.

When Peter came into the house, Jesus was the first to speak. "What do you think, Simon?" he asked. "From whom do the kings of the earth collect duty and taxes—from their own children or from others?"

"From others," Peter answered.

"Then the children are exempt," Jesus said to him. "But so that we may not cause offense, go to the lake and throw out your line. Take the first fish you catch; open its mouth and you will find a four-drachma coin. Take it and give it to them for my tax and yours."

LIFE LESSONS

Matthew is the only gospel writer who records this account about Peter being questioned concerning the temple tax. This tax was imposed by the Jewish leaders at the temple in Jerusalem. Exodus 30:11–16 explains that it was the people's responsibility to take care of their place of worship. In the Old Testament, paying this contribution was one of the people's primary connection points to God because contributing to the temple was part of their atonement.

In Matthew 12:6, Jesus has already explained to the people that He is greater than the temple—He *is* the Temple. You would think the Son of God would be exempt from the tax. Jesus is Lord over everything, yet He humbly submits to paying the tax *"so that we may not cause offense."* Jesus still pays the bill. He respects a different kind of authority, showing a graciousness when it's decent to do so and doesn't go against His own work, His purpose. He knows He's higher than it all, yet He does what is expected in order to make the temple leaders happy in this small thing.

Jesus sets a great example for us here. Just because God is our authority doesn't mean we can run around claiming that no one else has authority over us. We are still to submit, to a reasonable extent, to the authorities who have been set above us. We follow God, yes, but we also live under laws and rules within our society that provide for peace and order.

WHERE ARE YOU?

What points was Jesus communicating to Peter concerning His obligation toward the temple tax?

_____
_____
_____
_____

Why do you think Jesus provided for Peter's tax as well as for His own?

_____
_____
_____
_____

In what ways can you follow Jesus's example in this story by submitting to human authority while still living for God first?

_____
_____
_____
_____
_____

A PRAYER

Jesus, thank You for always being the perfect example for us. All I have to do is keep looking to You, and I will understand how this life is to be lived along the way, with humility and kindness. In Your name, amen.

DAY 71:
GREATNESS IN HUMILITY

SCRIPTURE READINGS

MATTHEW 18:1–5 (NLT)

About that time the disciples came to Jesus and asked, "Who is greatest in the Kingdom of Heaven?" Jesus called a little child to him and put the child among them. Then he said, "I tell you the truth, unless you turn from your sins and become like little children, you will never get into the Kingdom of Heaven. So anyone who becomes as humble as this little child is the greatest in the Kingdom of Heaven. And anyone who welcomes a little child like this on my behalf is welcoming me."

MARK 9:33–37 (NLT)

After they arrived at Capernaum and settled in a house, Jesus asked his disciples, "What were you discussing out on the road?" But they didn't answer, because they had been arguing about which of them was the greatest. He sat down, called the twelve disciples over to him, and said, "Whoever wants to be first must take last place and be the servant of everyone else." Then he put a little child among them. Taking the child in his arms, he said to them, "Anyone who welcomes a little child like this on my behalf welcomes me, and anyone who welcomes me welcomes not only me but also my Father who sent me."

SEE ALSO: LUKE 9:46–48

LIFE LESSONS

Small children don't have much control over their own lives. Even the everyday matters—what they eat, what their pastimes get to be, when they go to bed—are set for them. They're dependent on someone else to provide for them, take care of them, and guide them. And, for the most part, children accept this. It's not that they're perfect in submission—they still have flaws—it's that they realize their need, their powerlessness. They look to others to provide for them, and they surrender themselves to it.

When the disciples were arguing about who was the greatest, they received an answer that leaned in the opposite direction of what they wanted for themselves: the one who is childlike, the one who is a servant to others. Humility—not strength or achievements or charisma—is the answer. It is through humility that we enter the kingdom of heaven, and it's also through humility that we become great. Understanding that we need to rely entirely on God—that our successes are His and that He's the one providing—is crucial to moving forward in our faith. It means humbling ourselves and admitting that He alone is in charge. That is when God can do great things through us.

WHERE ARE YOU?

According to Jesus, what does it mean to be "great"?

_____

_____

_____

_____

_____

What was Jesus referring to when He said we need to become like little children?

_____

_____

_____

_____

_____

What do you have trouble giving over to God to take care of? How might you become more childlike in your attitude to help you give it over to Him?

_____

_____

_____

_____

_____

A PRAYER

Jesus, thank You for redefining greatness for us. Help me to come to You with childlike faith, ready to admit that I am powerless without You. I want to approach my relationship with You with humility so You can work through me in wonderful ways. In Your name, amen.

DAY 72:
PART OF THE FAMILY

SCRIPTURE READINGS

MARK 9:38–41 (NLT)

John said to Jesus, "Teacher, we saw someone using your name to cast out demons, but we told him to stop because he wasn't in our group."

"Don't stop him!" Jesus said. "No one who performs a miracle in my name will soon be able to speak evil of me. Anyone who is not against us is for us. If anyone gives you even a cup of water because you belong to the Messiah, I tell you the truth, that person will surely be rewarded."

LUKE 9:49–50 (NLT)

John said to Jesus, "Master, we saw someone using your name to cast out demons, but we told him to stop because he isn't in our group."

But Jesus said, "Don't stop him! Anyone who is not against you is for you."

LIFE LESSONS

Human beings like exclusivity. We like being part of something unique. We like feeling special. So, we create barriers against others, closing ourselves off from them with an "us versus them" mentality. But Jesus's message isn't meant to be exclusive. It's not supposed to cater to our feelings of "greatness." We should never use His message to keep people out.

The individual the disciples were talking about was doing the same things the disciples were doing—acting in the name of Jesus—and yet they wanted to stop him because he wasn't part of their group. Jesus corrected them. As long as we have the same goal of spreading the love of Jesus, we're part of the same group! Anyone acting with Jesus's love, kindness, and acceptance shouldn't be stopped or swayed from doing so. Anyone who loves Jesus, helps out the church, or promotes Jesus's message in some way, even if they are different from us, should be considered part of the family. Jesus clarified that all acts of service to Him are of equal significance, no matter who they come from. So, if you're ever feeling like you don't quite fit in anywhere, don't worry. You are already confirmed as being part of the group. Keep going!

WHERE ARE YOU?

What do you believe Jesus's message was in these passages?

_____

_____

_____

_____

_____

How should we treat other Christians even if they have different opinions from us or come from other church denominations or backgrounds?

_____

_____

_____

_____

_____

How do you think different groups and denominations can overcome the barriers that separate them?

_____

_____

_____

_____

_____

A PRAYER

Jesus, forgive us for grouping people into certain categories in our minds. Anyone who acts in love in Your name should be welcomed. Help me to be open-minded, to look for Your love demonstrated in others and accept them as they are. In Your name, amen.

DAY 73:
HOW ARE WE REPRESENTING CHRIST?

SCRIPTURE READINGS

MATTHEW 18:6–7 (NLT)

But if you cause one of these little ones who trusts in me to fall into sin, it would be better for you to have a large millstone tied around your neck and be drowned in the depths of the sea.

What sorrow awaits the world, because it tempts people to sin. Temptations are inevitable, but what sorrow awaits the person who does the tempting.

MARK 9:42 (NLT)

But if you cause one of these little ones who trusts in me to fall into sin, it would be better for you to be thrown into the sea with a large millstone hung around your neck.

LIFE LESSONS

It's inevitable that we're going to mess up sometimes. It's human nature. But it's one thing to stumble on our own walk with God; it's another thing to cause others to fall or prevent them from walking with Him altogether. You see, our words and actions can hinder other people from accepting Jesus (to the point of their not wanting to hear anything about Him) or from sticking around after they've found Him.

God takes it very seriously when we drive others away from Him. There are consequences for misleading people and misrepresenting Christ. Our actions have repercussions, and it's important to ask ourselves how we're representing Christ to others. Are we creating barriers to keep people out? Are we refusing to accept people as they are? Are we preaching God's grace? Are we acting in love?

WHERE ARE YOU?

How do you view the balance between being forgiven for sin and experiencing the consequences of one's actions?

_____

_____

_____

_____

_____

What kinds of actions—intentional or unintentional—might mislead others about Christ or cause them to stumble?

_____

_____

_____

_____

_____

What can we do to avoid causing others to be misled or to stumble?

_____

_____

_____

_____

_____

A PRAYER

Jesus, may my words and actions encourage others on their journey, not turn them away from You. Forgive me for the times I haven't represented You well, times I might have been a stumbling block for someone else. Help me to show others Your grace and love and to lift other people up. In Your name, amen.

DAY 74:
TEMPORAL VERSUS ETERNAL

SCRIPTURE READINGS

MATTHEW 18:8–9 (NIV)

If your hand or your foot causes you to stumble, cut it off and throw it away. It is better for you to enter life maimed or crip pled than to have two hands or two feet and be thrown into eternal fire. And if your eye causes you to stumble, gouge it out and throw it away. It is better for you to enter life with one eye than to have two eyes and be thrown into the fire of hell.

MARK 9:43–50 (MSG)

If your hand or your foot gets in God's way, chop it off and throw it away. You're better off maimed or lame and alive than the proud owner of two hands and two feet, godless in a furnace of eternal fire. And if your eye distracts you from God, pull it out and throw it away. You're better off one-eyed and alive than exercising your twenty-twenty vision from inside the fire of hell.

Everyone's going through a refining fire sooner or later, but you'll be well-preserved, protected from the eternal flames. Be preservatives yourselves. Preserve the peace.

LIFE LESSONS

First of all, don't be alarmed by these passages. Yes, these are graphic illustrations, but they are also hyperboles—extreme overstatements, meant to emphasize the fundamental truths behind the words. Scripture actually prohibits self-mutilation in at least four different Old Testament passages.

The point of this teaching is that nothing is more important than your relationship with Jesus and spending eternity with Him. Your hands, feet, eyes, job, hobbies, friends—none of these is worth losing your relationship with Christ. If any of them are pulling you away from Him, it would be better to lose them than to lose God. It would be a huge mistake to allow something temporal to keep you from something eternal.

WHERE ARE YOU?

Have any of your friends or associates been coming between you and God? How might you need to change your relationships to stay strong on your journey with Jesus?

_____

_____

_____

_____

_____

Have any of your hobbies or pastimes been drawing you away from God? Which activities might you need to give up to stay on course?

_____

_____

_____

_____

_____

Following along with the biblical analogy of the parts of our bodies that might cause us to stumble, what are your hands reaching out for in life right now? Where are your feet taking you? What are your eyes looking at? Are they drawing you closer to God?

_____

_____

_____

_____

_____

A PRAYER

Jesus, help me to see clearly whatever might be creating a wedge between me and You. Give me the strength to let go of anything that is pushing me away from You. Help me to choose the eternal over the temporary. In Your name, amen.

DAY 75:
EACH PERSON MATTERS

SCRIPTURE READING

MATTHEW 18:10–14 (NLT)

Beware that you don't look down on any of these little ones. For I tell you that in heaven their angels are always in the presence of my heavenly Father.

If a man has a hundred sheep and one of them wanders away, what will he do? Won't he leave the ninety-nine others on the hills and go out to search for the one that is lost? And if he finds it, I tell you the truth, he will rejoice over it more than over the ninety-nine that didn't wander away! In the same way, it is not my heavenly Father's will that even one of these little ones should perish.

LIFE LESSONS

We all need to make sure we don't fall into the trap of thinking we are better than others, especially those who have messed up, have veered off course, or haven't yet found God. Remember, our words and actions come from what's in our hearts, deep inside ourselves. If we have an attitude of pride or superiority toward other people, that attitude will start to seep into our actions.

We all fall down, we all make mistakes, we are all on a journey, and we are all human. When we start to feel superior to others, we need to check our hearts and realign them with God's heart before our actions start negatively affecting the people around us. Whenever someone comes back to God, regardless of the circumstances that took them far away from Him, we should always be excited about their return. We should always be ready to reach out and accept other people as equals because they are just as important to God as we are. Each person matters to Him, and we should care about those whom Jesus cares about and treat them accordingly—no matter where they are on their journey.

WHERE ARE YOU?

If a child were to ask you the point of Jesus's story about the lost sheep, what explanation would you give them?

_____

_____

_____

_____

_____

What promise does this story offer for each of us?

_____

_____

_____

_____

_____

How can we keep our mindset and our heart right so that we treat others properly?

_____

_____

_____

_____

_____

A PRAYER

Jesus, let my attitudes toward other people be pure. Keep pride out of my heart so I don't give in to the temptation to look down on others. I want to love like You love and care like You care. Help my thoughts and actions to be kind and accepting. In Your name, amen.

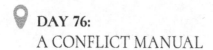

DAY 76:
A CONFLICT MANUAL

SCRIPTURE READING

MATTHEW 18:15–20 (NIV)

If your brother or sister sins, go and point out their fault, just between the two of you. If they listen to you, you have won them over. But if they will not listen, take one or two others along, so that "every matter may be established by the testimony of two or three witnesses." If they still refuse to listen, tell it to the church; and if they refuse to listen even to the church, treat them as you would a pagan or a tax collector.

Truly I tell you, whatever you bind on earth will be bound in heaven, and whatever you loose on earth will be loosed in heaven.

Again, truly I tell you that if two of you on earth agree about anything they ask for, it will be done for them by my Father in heaven. For where two or three gather in my name, there am I with them.

LIFE LESSONS

In this passage, Jesus provides us with a manual for dealing with conflict, and He's clear that the goal should always be restoration. Division can tear a community apart, even a community of faith; and, before you know it, people give up on the faith and walk away.

We have been talking about how God values each individual soul. If we are to be like Him, then we should put a huge value on straying sheep. We should seek to restore such people to the body of Christ, doing what we can to forgive, heal, and reconcile.

It's so easy to get this wrong when someone refuses to participate in restoration, but condemning, passing judgment, and giving up on them isn't the answer. Jesus still loved people when their lives were messy. He continued to invite them in, continued to be with them. They may not have been in His inner circle, but they mattered to Him.

Remember, we will all stray at some point. We need to think about how we would want someone to approach us in our weaker moments, when we're feeling defensive and far away from God. How would you want to be brought back to Christ? Keep that in mind when the next sheep goes astray.

WHERE ARE YOU?

When someone has done something wrong, do you usually approach them with a mindset of restoration or one of condemnation?

_____

_____

_____

_____

_____

Why do you think you approach them in that way?

_____

_____

_____

_____

_____

Does anything about your method of conflict resolution need to change? How can your attitudes, words, and actions be more Christlike when you talk with someone about a weakness or a failing?

_____

_____

_____

_____

_____

A PRAYER

Jesus, thank You for Your continual forgiveness. Thank You for restoring us every time we return to You. Help me to speak the truth in love to those who have strayed from You so they can experience forgiveness and healing. Give me wisdom for approaching conflicts effectively. In Your name, amen.

DAY 77:
THE LIMIT DOES NOT EXIST

SCRIPTURE READING

MATTHEW 18:21–35 (NIV)

Then Peter came to Jesus and asked, "Lord, how many times shall I forgive my brother or sister who sins against me? Up to seven times?"

Jesus answered, "I tell you, not seven times, but seventy-seven times.

"Therefore, the kingdom of heaven is like a king who wanted to settle accounts with his servants. As he began the settlement, a man who owed him ten thousand bags of gold was brought to him. Since he was not able to pay, the master ordered that he and his wife and his children and all that he had be sold to repay the debt.

"At this the servant fell on his knees before him. 'Be patient with me,' he begged, 'and I will pay back everything.' The servant's master took pity on him, canceled the debt and let him go.

"But when that servant went out, he found one of his fellow servants who owed him a hundred silver coins. He grabbed him and began to choke him. 'Pay back what you owe me!' he demanded.

"His fellow servant fell to his knees and begged him, 'Be patient with me, and I will pay it back.'

"But he refused. Instead, he went off and had the man thrown into prison until he could pay the debt. When the other servants saw what had happened, they were outraged and went and told their master everything that had happened.

"Then the master called the servant in. 'You wicked servant,' he said, 'I canceled all that debt of yours because you begged me to. Shouldn't you have had mercy on your fellow servant just as I had on you?' In anger his master handed him over to the jailers to be tortured, until he should pay back all he owed.

"This is how my heavenly Father will treat each of you unless you forgive your brother or sister from your heart."

LIFE LESSONS

When it comes to the number of times you are willing to forgive other people for their offenses, stop counting! There shouldn't be a cutoff number or a limit to forgiveness. Can you imagine if God kept track of how many times He forgave us and then stopped forgiving us after a certain number was reached? We would all be in a rough spot if that were the case!

God forgives all our sins, both large and small. His forgiveness is unlimited—and ours should be as well. The size of the offense or debt does not matter, and this passage reiterates that. The man in the story never could have paid off his debt to the king—and that's the point! God's forgiveness toward us is limitless, and we should pay it forward. Forgiven people should forgive people.

WHERE ARE YOU?

Has someone ever not forgiven you for something you did? How did that make you feel?

Have you ever felt like someone's offense was too big for you to forgive? How did you end up dealing with that situation? Does it still need resolution?

How can we focus more on the forgiveness that God has granted us so we can extend forgiveness to others?

_____

_____

_____

_____

_____

A PRAYER

Jesus, I don't want to be like the unforgiving man in Your parable. Help me to forgive as You have forgiven me: without counting others' sins, without weighing the size of their debts to decide if they're too large to forgive, without ceasing to forgive altogether. Give me the strength and will to forgive when it's hard, so I can keep loving others as You do. In Your name, amen.

A DIFFERENT KIND OF CLOCK

SCRIPTURE READING
....

JOHN 7:1–9 (NLT)

After this, Jesus traveled around Galilee. He wanted to stay out of Judea, where the Jewish leaders were plotting his death. But soon it was time for the Jewish Festival of Shelters, and Jesus' brothers said to him, "Leave here and go to Judea, where your followers can see your miracles! You can't become famous if you hide like this! If you can do such wonderful things, show yourself to the world!" For even his brothers didn't believe in him.

Jesus replied, "Now is not the right time for me to go, but you can go anytime. The world can't hate you, but it does hate me because I accuse it of doing evil. You go on. I'm not going to this festival, because my time has not yet come." After saying these things, Jesus remained in Galilee.

LIFE LESSONS
....

Timing is everything, and, according to Ecclesiastes 3:1, there is a season for everything, *"a time for every activity under heaven"* (NLT). We can't rush time; we can only accept it.

Jesus was willing to wait for God's schedule. His brothers wanted Him to go to the annual Festival of Shelters (also referred to as the Feast of Booths), but the religious leaders in Judea wanted to kill Him. That's a pretty good reason not to go to the festival! Jesus knew it wasn't the right moment to face the leaders. It would have interfered with God's overall plan.

We tend to let the clock of this world dictate our schedules and expectations. We want life to happen when we want it to happen. We want progress right away, whether it's a type of change, success, or a happy relationship. But we can't force any of those things to occur. Instead, we have to take them as they come. We have to accept the reality that some things take time, we will be stuck in some seasons longer than others, and all seasons come and go.

It's the same with our spiritual walk. We can't rush it. We can't sit there watching the clock, so to speak, or we'll miss what God is doing with us *now*. It's essential to trust His timing. We will be ready to progress when He says we're ready. We will be stronger some days than others, closer to God some days than others. But as we grow, we will develop a deeper relationship with Him. So grasp hold of each season of your life and live it the best you can, knowing that, at some point, that season will come to an end and a new one will greet you.

WHERE ARE YOU?

How would you describe your current season of life in general? How would you describe your current spiritual season?

_____

_____

_____

_____

Do you find it difficult to wait for God's timing? Why or why not?

_____

_____

_____

_____

How does a seasonal approach to life give you hope for tomorrow?

_____

_____

_____

_____

A PRAYER

Jesus, You Yourself had to trust in Your Father's timing and plan. Help me to trust not only Your will but also Your perfect timing. Give me patience for the many seasons in my life. Grant me an eternal perspective for my walk with You. In Your name, amen.

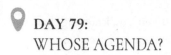 DAY 79:
WHOSE AGENDA?

SCRIPTURE READING

LUKE 9:51–56 (NLT)

As the time drew near for him to ascend to heaven, Jesus resolutely set out for Jerusalem. He sent messengers ahead to a Samaritan village to prepare for his arrival. But the people of the village did not welcome Jesus because he was on his way to Jerusalem. When James and John saw this, they said to Jesus, "Lord, should we call down fire from heaven to burn them up?" But Jesus turned and rebuked them. So they went on to another village.

LIFE LESSONS

At this point, Jesus was determined to go to Jerusalem, and His disciples misinterpreted this objective to mean that Jesus was about to take His throne as King. Not only did the disciples misunderstand, but they also jumped the gun quite a bit—they were ready to start conquering, to overthrow and destroy their enemies right then. It's as if they had already forgotten the purpose of Jesus's message. Their minds were focused on what they wanted, what they expected, not on what Jesus was teaching them. Their motives fit their *own* agenda for God's kingdom, not His.

Jesus's disciples thought they knew what was about to happen, but they were way off—Jesus was en route to Jerusalem with such determination because He was headed to the cross. The cross would lead to an empty tomb, which would lead to a throne—but not the immediate earthly throne the disciples were thinking of. They just wanted the throne; they wanted to skip to the end.

Similarly, we have to be careful not to succumb to focusing on what we want to get out of our relationship with God and therefore lose sight of what He's doing with us and with His purposes for the world.

WHERE ARE YOU?

What different perspectives about Jesus's mission on earth did Jesus and His disciples have?

_____

_____

_____

_____

_____

In your relationship with Jesus, have you been trying to promote your own agenda? Have you been pressing for what you want over what He wants?

_____

_____

_____

_____

_____

Where do you think God is leading you in your life right now?

_____

_____

_____

_____

_____

A PRAYER

Jesus, don't ever let me forget what Your message, Your sacrifice, and our relationship are about. They're not about what I want. Whenever I try to turn my relationship with You into merely what I desire, help me to stop right there and listen to You, allowing You to redirect me. While the world seeks titles, success, and its own agendas, keep my eyes fixed on following You. In Your name, amen.

DAY 80:
THE COST OF DISCIPLESHIP

SCRIPTURE READINGS

MATTHEW 8:19–22 (CEV)

A teacher of the Law of Moses came up to him and said, "Teacher, I'll go anywhere with you!"

Jesus replied, "Foxes have dens, and birds have nests. But the Son of Man doesn't have a place to call his own."

Another disciple said to Jesus, "Lord, let me wait till I bury my father."

Jesus answered, "Follow me, and let the dead bury their dead."

LUKE 9:57–62 (CEV)

Along the way someone said to Jesus, "I'll follow you anywhere!"

Jesus said, "Foxes have dens, and birds have nests, but the Son of Man doesn't have a place to call his own."

Jesus told someone else to come with him. But the man said, "Lord, let me wait until I bury my father."

Jesus answered, "Let the dead take care of the dead, while you go and tell about God's kingdom."

Then someone said to Jesus, "I want to follow you, Lord, but first let me go back and take care of things at home."

Jesus answered, "Anyone who starts plowing and keeps looking back isn't worth a thing to God's kingdom!"

LIFE LESSONS

It's easy to be vocal about our enthusiasm for following God, but living up to that profession can be a different story. In this passage, Jesus comes back to a familiar topic: the cost of discipleship. It is a lesson He teaches over and over again. People may make bold claims about following Him, but the proof is seen in their commitment, their decisions, and their actions.

In these passages, three people apparently put off following Jesus. The first person was challenged by Jesus about the road to come. Jesus wouldn't be stopping and settling down at any point—He was on a long, never-ending trek, and the terrain could be rough. Was this person willing to follow Jesus under those circumstances? The second person was dealing with misplaced priorities. Going home wouldn't be a small delay; it would be a long delay. This individual clearly wasn't ready to leave certain commitments behind. The third person just wasn't prepared to leave his home and everything he knew behind. But the truth we see in all three of these examples is this: anything that holds us back from our relationship with God isn't worth our time.

We can always find reasons to delay truly committing to our journey with Jesus. There will always be people we don't want to leave behind, projects we want to complete, and things we're expected to do by those around us. Always. It's up to us to choose our journey with Jesus over these barriers, and to choose it now—not later. Or it might never happen.

WHERE ARE YOU?

What has it cost you to follow Jesus?

_____

_____

_____

_____

_____

Do you find yourself delaying any aspects of your relationship with Jesus or what you think God wants you to do? If so, why?

_____

_____

_____

_____

_____

In what specific ways can you follow God into all that He has for you?

A PRAYER

Jesus, as I count the cost of following You, I know there is no cost too great for the privilege of being with You. Help me to keep my priorities in line. Let my actions live up to my words. In Your name, amen.

DAY 81:
THE TURNING POINT

SCRIPTURE READING

JOHN 7:10–24 (CEV)

After Jesus' brothers had gone to the festival, he went secretly, without telling anyone.

During the festival the leaders of the people looked for Jesus and asked, "Where is he?" The crowds even got into an argument about him. Some were saying, "Jesus is a good man," while others were saying, "He is lying to everyone." But the people were afraid of their leaders, and none of them talked in public about him.

When the festival was about half over, Jesus went into the temple and started teaching. The leaders were surprised and said, "How does this man know so much? He has never been taught!"

Jesus replied:

> *I am not teaching something I thought up. What I teach comes from the one who sent me. If you really want to obey God, you will know if what I teach comes from God or from me. If I wanted to bring honor to myself, I would speak for myself. But I want to honor the one who sent me. This is why I tell the truth and not a lie. Didn't Moses give you the Law? Yet none of you obey it! So why do you want to kill me?*

The crowd replied, "You're crazy! What makes you think someone wants to kill you?"

Jesus answered:

> *I worked one miracle, and it amazed you. Moses commanded you to circumcise your sons. But it wasn't really Moses who gave you this command. It was your ancestors, and even on the Sabbath you circumcise your sons in order to obey the Law of Moses. Why are you angry with me for making someone completely well on the Sabbath? Don't judge by appearances. Judge by what is right.*

LIFE LESSONS

The Festival of Shelters, or Booths, is a Jewish celebration commemorating the years that God's people spent in tents in the wilderness, traveling toward the promised land. Jerusalem would fill with tents as people honored their heritage, and the feast was perfectly timed to take place at harvest. It was a joyful occasion to celebrate God's provision through the harvest and to remember His past protection and provision.

Each day during this feast, people would follow the priest to the Pool of Siloam while chanting psalms. The priest would dip his golden pitcher into the pool, and the people would recite Isaiah 12:3: *"With joy you will drink deeply from the fountain of salvation!"* (NLT). Then the people would follow the priest back to the altar, where the water would be poured out as an offering to the Lord.

Jesus's teachings at this festival mark the beginning of the end for Him in terms of His road to the cross. He's finally teaching truths blatantly, laying them all out plainly. Even previously, although people tended to like Jesus in general—thinking of Him as a good person who healed the sick and fed people—they didn't always like some of His more intense messages. This is a turning point in His ministry. From here on out, the opposition will get worse and worse.

WHERE ARE YOU?

How do people's opinions about Jesus in this passage compare to what people think of Jesus today?

_____

_____

_____

_____

In terms of the big picture, what is going on here between Jesus and the religious leaders and the rest of the crowd?

_____

_____

_____

_____

Jesus told the people, "Don't judge by appearances. Judge by what is right." In what way might you have judged someone's action by its appearance rather than taking time to evaluate that action by what is right according to God's character and Word?

_____

_____

_____

_____

_____

A PRAYER

Jesus, You poured out Your life so that I could *"drink deeply from the fountain of salvation."* Thank You for Your sacrifice, which makes salvation possible. In Your name, amen.

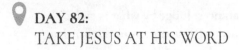

DAY 82:
TAKE JESUS AT HIS WORD

SCRIPTURE READING

John 7:25–36 (NLT)

Some of the people who lived in Jerusalem started to ask each other, "Isn't this the man they are trying to kill? But here he is, speaking in public, and they say nothing to him. Could our leaders possibly believe that he is the Messiah? But how could he be? For we know where this man comes from. When the Messiah comes, he will simply appear; no one will know where he comes from."

While Jesus was teaching in the Temple, he called out, "Yes, you know me, and you know where I come from. But I'm not here on my own. The one who sent me is true, and you don't know him. But I know him because I come from him, and he sent me to you." Then the leaders tried to arrest him; but no one laid a hand on him, because his time had not yet come.

Many among the crowds at the Temple believed in him. "After all," they said, "would you expect the Messiah to do more miraculous signs than this man has done?"

When the Pharisees heard that the crowds were whispering such things, they and the leading priests sent Temple guards to arrest Jesus. But Jesus told them, "I will be with you only a little longer. Then I will return to the one who sent me. You will search for me but not find me. And you cannot go where I am going."

The Jewish leaders were puzzled by this statement. "Where is he planning to go?" they asked. "Is he thinking of leaving the country and going to the Jews in other lands? Maybe he will even teach the Greeks! What does he mean when he says, 'You will search for me but not find me,' and 'You cannot go where I am going'?"

LIFE LESSONS

Jesus's claim to be the Messiah divided crowds then and still divides them to this day. Many people choose not to believe in Him. Many other people choose to believe only in part, picking which aspects of His teachings they approve of. This can be especially true of religious leaders. They preach parts of His message but refuse to take all of Him as He is. Others still hang tightly to only the early Scriptures, continuing to wait for a Savior who has already arrived. For many, the desire to be right, to affirm that everything they've held dear in the past is true, is their downfall.

It is tragic when devoted religious people miss the Messiah because of their narrow perspective. They hold their limited wisdom and their traditions so closely that they can't quite make room in their hearts to believe in Jesus. Even in this story, the religious leaders had the Old Testament Scriptures but failed to receive the One about whom those Scriptures so plainly prophesied. And they were seeing Him with their own two eyes.

Again, sometimes it's easier for those with fewer preconceptions to believe in Jesus, to take in His message. They have less standing in their way. They can accept His statements more readily. But whether we're bringing more or less into our relationship with Jesus, we all need to drop our previously constructed expectations—whatever we think we know—and be ready to take Jesus at His word.

WHERE ARE YOU?

Are you presently having difficulty accepting any of Jesus's statements or teachings? Which ones in particular have been harder for you to process?

Do you feel you accept Jesus entirely as He is? Why or why not?

Do you have any reservations about God that you're still hanging on to from your past and want to resolve? Talk over your reservations with a trusted Christian friend, mentor, or pastor and ask them to pray with you about these concerns.

_____

_____

_____

_____

_____

A PRAYER

Jesus, I pray for those who hold so tightly to what they think they already know that they refuse to see who You really are. Please open their hearts so they can experience You. I want to accept You exactly as You are. Help me, too, to release any expectations about You that may get in the way of this. In Your name, amen.

DAY 83:
TO QUENCH OUR THIRST

SCRIPTURE READING

JOHN 7:37–44 (NLT)

On the last day, the climax of the festival, Jesus stood and shouted to the crowds, "Anyone who is thirsty may come to me! Anyone who believes in me may come and drink! For the Scriptures declare, 'Rivers of living water will flow from his heart.'" (When he said "living water," he was speaking of the Spirit, who would be given to everyone believing in him. But the Spirit had not yet been given, because Jesus had not yet entered into his glory.)

When the crowds heard him say this, some of them declared, "Surely this man is the Prophet we've been expecting." Others said, "He is the Messiah." Still others said, "But he can't be! Will the Messiah come from Galilee? For the Scriptures clearly state that the Messiah will be born of the royal line of David, in Bethlehem, the village where King David was born." So the crowd was divided about him. Some even wanted him arrested, but no one laid a hand on him.

LIFE LESSONS

In the Festival of Shelters, or Booths, the priest brought a golden pitcher from the Pool of Siloam to the temple altar for seven straight days. On the seventh day, the priest circled the altar seven times. (In the Bible, seven is the number of completion. It is also reminiscent of the seven times the nation of Israel marched around the walls of Jericho.) This priest was then joined by another priest who carried wine on the seventh and final circuit around the altar. Both priests raised their pitchers, stopping for a dramatic pause. This was the highest point of celebration of the entire weeklong feast.

It was exactly at this moment that Jesus stood and spoke the words, *"Anyone who is thirsty may come to me!"* He purposefully chose that poignant moment to make this statement and make His point.

Jesus offers water for an otherwise unquenchable thirst—to fill the emptiness and longing inside us and to bring us peace. All we have to do is go to Him and drink.

WHERE ARE YOU?

After saying that everyone who believes in Him may come and drink, Jesus made the following statement: "Rivers of living water will flow from his heart." What do you think He meant by this?

_____
_____
_____
_____
_____

On a scale of one to ten, how thirsty are you for Jesus as your Living Water?

_____
_____
_____
_____
_____

How might you increase that thirst?

_____
_____
_____
_____
_____

A PRAYER

Jesus, thank You for always being there for me. Help me to hunger and thirst for You. Fill my heart with You. Satisfy my hunger with Your Word and my thirst with Your presence. In Your name, amen.

DAY 84:
STANDING OUR GROUND

SCRIPTURE READING

JOHN 7:45–53 (NLT)

When the Temple guards returned without having arrested Jesus, the leading priests and Pharisees demanded, "Why didn't you bring him in?"

"We have never heard anyone speak like this!" the guards responded.

"Have you been led astray, too?" the Pharisees mocked. "Is there a single one of us rulers or Pharisees who believes in him? This foolish crowd follows him, but they are ignorant of the law. God's curse is on them!"

Then Nicodemus, the leader who had met with Jesus earlier, spoke up. "Is it legal to convict a man before he is given a hearing?" he asked.

They replied, "Are you from Galilee, too? Search the Scriptures and see for yourself—no prophet ever comes from Galilee!"

Then the meeting broke up, and everybody went home.

LIFE LESSONS

Speaking up for what we believe in can be a lonely road. Whether the matter is about God, our rights, or other people's rights, it automatically puts us in a precarious position where we have to weigh the costs of speaking out.

Nicodemus had gone to meet with Jesus previously, but under cover of darkness. Now, just speaking up and talking reasonably about Jesus's already-established rights in front of his religious peers puts him at risk. This is no small thing. It could cost him his position and his place in society, and it could possibly instigate the anger of very powerful men against him.

It can be terrifying to stand our ground when something important is at stake. Even smaller situations, like risking the judgment of a new friend, can be difficult. But our actions reflect our hearts. If we're abandoning our values and our beliefs at the first sign of resistance, what does that say about the condition of our hearts? Are we really living out what we believe?

WHERE ARE YOU?

When has someone stood up for you or your rights?

_____

_____

_____

_____

When have you stood up for someone else in this way? Was it difficult? Why or why not?

_____

_____

_____

_____

In what ways have you been supportive of those around you lately? How might you encourage someone this week by coming alongside them with assistance?

_____

_____

_____

_____

A PRAYER

Jesus, give me the strength to stand up for You and for others, and let me know You are with me, standing next to me. Don't let me abandon my values or run away when I'm under pressure or worried about the consequences. I want to unashamedly follow You. You are worth more than anything else in this world. In Your name, amen.

DAY 85:
LOOK AT YOURSELF

SCRIPTURE READING

JOHN 8:1–11 (NLT)

Jesus returned to the Mount of Olives, but early the next morning he was back again at the Temple. A crowd soon gathered, and he sat down and taught them. As he was speaking, the teachers of religious law and the Pharisees brought a woman who had been caught in the act of adultery. They put her in front of the crowd.

"Teacher," they said to Jesus, "this woman was caught in the act of adultery. The law of Moses says to stone her. What do you say?"

They were trying to trap him into saying something they could use against him, but Jesus stooped down and wrote in the dust with his finger. They kept demanding an answer, so he stood up again and said, "All right, but let the one who has never sinned throw the first stone!" Then he stooped down again and wrote in the dust.

When the accusers heard this, they slipped away one by one, beginning with the oldest, until only Jesus was left in the middle of the crowd with the woman. Then Jesus stood up again and said to the woman, "Where are your accusers? Didn't even one of them condemn you?"

"No, Lord," she said.

And Jesus said, "Neither do I. Go and sin no more."

LIFE LESSONS

None of us likes being the recipient of negative attention or judgment, but we tend to be pretty good at dishing it out toward others. Maybe we're just trying to get the attention off us or feel better about ourselves. Perhaps the reason for this is that our walk with God hasn't been great lately, so we're playing the comparison game to feel better. Maybe we tell ourselves that our own blunders were less public, affected less people around us, or are considered to be not as bad according to the perceptions of society. In whatever manner we justify it, we find a way to make ourselves come out on top.

Under the law, the penalty for adultery was stoning, so the religious leaders and Pharisees brought the woman who had been caught in adultery to Jesus to trap Him with a question. Jesus couldn't deny the existence of the law, so she would have to be stoned, which would be contrary to much of the message He had been teaching about forgiveness of sin. But everyone else there had sins that hadn't been publicly brought before the law. Jesus knew this. Instead of telling them not to stone the woman, He offered a new perspective: He reminded them of their own downfalls, their own sins, and also of their humanity.

When we stop focusing on others and judging them, it generally means we're left to take a hard look at ourselves. And that can be difficult to do. But Jesus's message is about God's love for us and His forgiveness of our sins—which we are to freely extend to others. This includes loving and forgiving ourselves.

WHERE ARE YOU?

Do you find it easier to point out the sins of others than to look at your own faults? Why or why not?

What rocks of judgment toward others are you currently holding on to that you need to drop?

Is there anything you need to forgive yourself for?

_____

_____

_____

_____

_____

A PRAYER

Lord Jesus, thank You for the love You show us and the forgiveness You provide for us. Help me to drop my critical attitude toward others and pick up Your love for them. Help me to take a hard look at my own failings and sins but then confess those failings and sins to You, receive Your forgiveness—and extend love and forgiveness toward myself as well. In Your name, amen.

DAY 86:
A BEACON IN THE NIGHT

SCRIPTURE READING

....

JOHN 8:12–30 (NLT)

Jesus spoke to the people once more and said, "I am the light of the world. If you follow me, you won't have to walk in darkness, because you will have the light that leads to life."

The Pharisees replied, "You are making those claims about yourself! Such testimony is not valid." Jesus told them, "These claims are valid even though I make them about myself. For I know where I came from and where I am going, but you don't know this about me. You judge me by human standards, but I do not judge anyone. And if I did, my judgment would be correct in every respect because I am not alone. The Father who sent me is with me. Your own law says that if two people agree about something, their witness is accepted as fact. I am one witness, and my Father who sent me is the other."

"Where is your father?" they asked. Jesus answered, "Since you don't know who I am, you don't know who my Father is. If you knew me, you would also know my Father." Jesus made these statements while he was teaching in the section of the Temple known as the Treasury. But he was not arrested, because his time had not yet come. Later Jesus said to them again, "I am going away. You will search for me but will die in your sin. You cannot come where I am going." The people asked, "Is he planning to commit suicide? What does he mean, 'You cannot come where I am going'?" Jesus continued, "You are from below; I am from above. You belong to this world; I do not. That is why I said that you will die in your sins; for unless you believe that I am who I claim to be, you will die in your sins."

"Who are you?" they demanded. Jesus replied, "The one I have always claimed to be. I have much to say about you and much to condemn, but I won't. For I say only what I have heard from the one who sent me, and he is completely truthful." But they still didn't understand that he was talking about his Father.

So Jesus said, "When you have lifted up the Son of Man on the cross, then you will understand that I am he. I do nothing on my own but say only what the Father taught me. And the one who sent me is with me—he has not deserted me. For I always do what pleases him." Then many who heard him say these things believed in him.

LIFE LESSONS

We live in a dark world. We've all felt it pressing in on us at some point. We've felt lost and aimless, hopeless and searching. But Jesus tells us He is the Light of the World. Not *a* light, but *the* Light.

God provides daily light in our lives primarily in two ways: through our reading of His Scriptures and through the enlightenment and guidance of His Holy Spirit. In Psalm 119:105, the psalmist declared, *"Your word is a lamp to guide my feet and a light for my path"* (NLT). In John 16:13, Jesus affirmed, *"When the Spirit of truth comes, he will guide you into all truth"* (NLT). God's Word guides our steps and gives us the essentials, a foundation, to work with, and then His Spirit brings understanding, illuminating those truths in our lives.

Every day, Jesus is there for us to look to, to count on, to reach out to. We might sometimes trip in the dark, lose sight of Him, and wander off for a bit, but He will still be there, standing before us: a beacon in the night, waiting for us to look up at Him again.

WHERE ARE YOU?

Why is Jesus uniquely qualified to testify about Himself?

How has your walk with Jesus brought light to your life?

Are there any dark areas of your life that Jesus's light needs to expose? When you identify those areas, bring them to Jesus and ask Him to illuminate them with His truth and bring freedom and healing to you.

_____

_____

_____

_____

_____

A PRAYER

Jesus, You are the Light of the World. Please illuminate my path. Help me to keep my eyes on Your light so that I can walk down the road of Your perfect will for my life. Help me to look back up at You when I've stumbled and gotten off track. Thank You for waiting patiently for me so that I will never have to walk in darkness and never be alone. In Your name, amen.

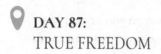

DAY 87:
TRUE FREEDOM

SCRIPTURE READING
....

JOHN 8:31–41 (NLT)

Jesus said to the people who believed in him, "You are truly my disciples if you remain faithful to my teachings. And you will know the truth, and the truth will set you free."

"But we are descendants of Abraham," they said. "We have never been slaves to anyone. What do you mean, 'You will be set free'?"

Jesus replied, "I tell you the truth, everyone who sins is a slave of sin. A slave is not a permanent member of the family, but a son is part of the family forever. So if the Son sets you free, you are truly free. Yes, I realize that you are descendants of Abraham. And yet some of you are trying to kill me because there's no room in your hearts for my message. I am telling you what I saw when I was with my Father. But you are following the advice of your father."

"Our father is Abraham!" they declared.

"No," Jesus replied, "for if you were really the children of Abraham, you would follow his example. Instead, you are trying to kill me because I told you the truth, which I heard from God. Abraham never did such a thing. No, you are imitating your real father."

They replied, "We aren't illegitimate children! God himself is our true Father."

LIFE LESSONS
....

When we continually choose this world over God, we become trapped in it. It pulls us in. If we think we're above its control, a time will come that will show us we're not. None of us is in control of it. When we choose the world, our greed tends to grow, our addictions tend to get stronger, our lies create more lies. What might feel like freedom for a while...isn't.

If you've ever done something wrong and felt the crushing weight of regret and worry, if you've ever lied and then told a chain of further lies to cover up the first one, if you've ever been addicted to anything and felt like you couldn't get out of its trap no matter what you did, then you understand clearly what it means to feel enslaved to sin. Whether it feels that way to you or not, apart from Christ, we *are* slaves to sin—both to its consequences here on earth and in terms of our separation from God in the long run. Without Jesus, our earthly desires and selfishness take over. We feel like we don't need God, that we can do this on our own. We start to think that true freedom consists in making our own decisions, potentially even defying God. But, again, that's not freedom. It traps us even more in our problems—sets us in an even deeper hole that we can't get out of without help.

Whether we want to admit it or not, we can't free ourselves from this slavery to sin. Our freedom is found in letting go of the hard grip we have on our life and admitting that we don't really have control over it, that we need God. It's found in accepting the truth that the only way out is through Jesus. It's found in receiving God's forgiveness of our sins through Christ. Sometimes we have to remind ourselves of these things again and again because they are the only way to stay truly free.

WHERE ARE YOU?

What did Jesus tell the people was keeping them from being children of God?

_____

_____

_____

_____

_____

What did Jesus say would lead to our knowing the truth and thereby being set free from sin?

_____

_____

_____

_____

_____

How does knowing God as your Father deepen your personal walk with Him?

_____

_____

_____

_____

_____

A PRAYER

God, thank You for forgiving my sins and setting me free. Help me to stay grounded in the knowledge that You are the only source of true freedom. Help me to continue loosening my grip on the world. Thank You for guiding me to the truth and taking me in as a member of Your family. In Jesus's name, amen.

DAY 88:
LIKE FATHER, LIKE SON

SCRIPTURE READING

JOHN 8:42–47 (NLT)

Jesus told them, "If God were your Father, you would love me, because I have come to you from God. I am not here on my own, but he sent me. Why can't you understand what I am saying? It's because you can't even hear me! For you are the children of your father the devil, and you love to do the evil things he does. He was a murderer from the beginning. He has always hated the truth, because there is no truth in him. When he lies, it is consistent with his character; for he is a liar and the father of lies. So when I tell the truth, you just naturally don't believe me! Which of you can truthfully accuse me of sin? And since I am telling you the truth, why don't you believe me? Anyone who belongs to God listens gladly to the words of God. But you don't listen because you don't belong to God."

LIFE LESSONS

We all naturally inherit traits from our biological family, for better or for worse. In our Scripture reading, where Jesus teaches about belonging to a spiritual family, there's a clear distinction between the source of the "better or worse."

Even in the spiritual realm, Jesus says we all have a father—either God or Satan. Throughout our lives, our actions will imitate this father, and when we die, our spiritual inheritance will be directly related to who our father is. Jesus can tell who the father of these people is by their comments and actions. If God were their Father, they would love and accept His Son.

As we spend more time with God, we become more like Him. Not only in our actions, but also in our heart, our perspectives, and our understanding. If we're following our Father, it should be reflected in our lives as we gradually take on His traits.

WHERE ARE YOU?

In general, what do you think are your best traits?

What aspects of God's character are strongest in you?

What spiritual trait would you like to experience growth in?

A PRAYER

Father God, thank You for taking me in as Your own through the sacrifice of Your Son. I am blessed beyond measure to call You Father. Help me to continually become more like You. I love You. In Jesus's name, amen.

HONORING THE FATHER

SCRIPTURE READING

JOHN 8:48–55 (NLT)

The people retorted, "You Samaritan devil! Didn't we say all along that you were possessed by a demon?"

"No," Jesus said, "I have no demon in me. For I honor my Father—and you dishonor me. And though I have no wish to glorify myself, God is going to glorify me. He is the true judge. I tell you the truth, anyone who obeys my teaching will never die!"

The people said, "Now we know you are possessed by a demon. Even Abraham and the prophets died, but you say, 'Anyone who obeys my teaching will never die!' Are you greater than our father Abraham? He died, and so did the prophets. Who do you think you are?"

Jesus answered, "If I want glory for myself, it doesn't count. But it is my Father who will glorify me. You say, 'He is our God,' but you don't even know him. I know him. If I said otherwise, I would be as great a liar as you! But I do know him and obey him."

LIFE LESSONS

The fifth commandment, recorded in Exodus 20:12, is, *"Honor your father and mother"* (NLT, MSG). Whether or not we grew up in the church, we've all probably heard this commandment at some point in our lives. Valuing obedience to one's parents and elders is engrained in many cultures across the globe. Jesus exemplified this command to perfection. And in the first five books of the New Testament, He mentioned the topic of "father" 213 times. The designation of "Father" in reference to God was extremely important to Him.

Luke 23:34 records what many people believe were the first words Jesus spoke on the cross: *"Father, forgive them, for they don't know what they are doing"* (NLT). Then, in Luke 23:46, Jesus's final words, right before His last breath, were, *"Father, I entrust my spirit into your hands!"* (NLT).

Jesus did *everything* in obedience to His Father. He continually reached out to God, communicating with Him every step of the way. It was a relationship He valued and honored. We have the privilege of sharing a relationship with

God as well. It might seem a little strange at first to refer to God as Father, but using that term is a good way to reach out to Him as you would to a trusted parent, accepting that He cares about you more than you can know.

WHERE ARE YOU?

How is or was your relationship with your parents? Did you find it hard as a child to obey them? Why or why not?

_____

_____

_____

_____

_____

When do you find it hardest to obey God? Why do you think this is the case?

_____

_____

_____

_____

_____

In what ways can you honor God as your Father?

_____

_____

_____

_____

_____

A PRAYER

Jesus, thank You for showing us so clearly the relationship we can have with God. Your obedience to Him saved all of us; this is something we can never repay. Help my personal walk with the Father to imitate Yours. In Your name, amen.

DAY 90:
BEFORE AND AFTER, NOW AND FOREVER

SCRIPTURE READING

JOHN 8:56–59 (NLT)

[Jesus said,] *"Your father Abraham rejoiced as he looked forward to my coming. He saw it and was glad."*

The people said, "You aren't even fifty years old. How can you say you have seen Abraham?"

Jesus answered, "I tell you the truth, before Abraham was even born, I am!" At that point they picked up stones to throw at him. But Jesus was hidden from them and left the Temple.

LIFE LESSONS

Jesus has always existed and will always exist. In Colossians 1:17, Paul says, *"He existed before anything else, and he holds all creation together"* (NLT). Again, not only is Jesus before all things, but He will be here forever—from before the creation of the world to long after this version of the earth has come to an end.

Jesus will also never cease to be with you. He's been with you since the beginning and will continue to see you through every high and low point: every tear, every celebration, every loss, every increase. He will be there for it *all*. Never doubt that You can run to Him with anything, big or small. Remember, He came down to earth—and ultimately the cross—to *save*. And He came for all of us. He came for you. He wants to spend eternity with you. You just have to receive Him.

WHERE ARE YOU?

What do you think the crowd thought of Jesus when He declared, "Before Abraham was even born, I am!"? Why did the people want to stone Him?

_____

_____

_____

_____

_____

How is Jesus "holding all things together" for you during your journey with Him?

_____

_____

_____

_____

_____

At this point in your journey, can you define where you are in your relationship with Jesus?

_____

_____

_____

_____

_____

A PRAYER

Jesus, You are Alpha and Omega, the beginning and the end. You are not confined by time or space. You alone are the great I AM, and I know You'll continue to hold me in Your hand as I take my journey through this life. Thank You for all that You are and all that You do. In Your name, amen.

CONCLUSION

Congratulations for completing the second leg of this scriptural journey with Jesus! If you're going through all four Life Along the Way devotional books in order, you've just reached the halfway point. We hope your understanding of Jesus's life, truth, and role in your journey has become clearer each day.

You've now seen the incredible power of Jesus at work. You've witnessed His healings and watched the lives of His followers switch course altogether. Over and over again, you've observed people accept God's promises that change is possible and that they are worthy of love and a better life. We hope that you carry these promises of God's transforming power in your own heart as you walk through each day. You, too, are worthy of love and capable of being healed, and you are standing on a path with so many opportunities to progress and grow.

If you'd like to keep walking with us to understand the depths of Jesus's compassionate heart and how we can be an extension of His love for other people, be sure to pick up the third book in the Life Along the Way Series: *Jesus Through Us: Following His Example in Love and Service*. We are not without purpose on this earth, and this book is a perfect opportunity to learn from the very best Teacher how to radically love God and others.

And it might not just change your life but the lives of those around you as well....

CONTRIBUTORS TO THE LIFE ALONG THE WAY SERIES BY JOURNEYWISE

JourneyWise began as the passion project of Dr. Shane Stanford, a Methodist minister and author, and Dr. Ronnie Kent, a board-certified pediatrician and behavioral health specialist. These men, whose Christ-centered friendship and fellowship began nearly forty years ago, wanted to create a platform that would allow leading Christian thinkers, teachers, pastors, and content creators to share insights that would enable people to find their identity in Christ. Its faith-based media network helps people from all walks of life sit at the feet of Jesus and receive life from His Word. JourneyWise is part of The Moore-West Center for Applied Theology, which aims to train laity in biblical literacy, theological dialogue, apologetics, and critical thinking, and in serving through applied theology. It was founded for the purpose of equipping and engaging others to "love Jesus and love like Jesus" in the world. The Life Along the Way Series was developed to help fulfill that mission.

CONTRIBUTORS:

Dr. Shane Stanford is the founder and CEO of The Moore-West Center for Applied Theology, as well as the president of JourneyWise, The Moore-West Center's faith-based media network. Along with pastoring congregations in Florida, North Carolina, Mississippi, and Tennessee for more than thirty years, Shane served as host of *The Methodist Hour* on TV and radio, reaching more than thirty million homes nationwide. He was awarded an honorary doctorate in divinity from Asbury Seminary, and he holds a master of divinity degree in theology and ethics from Duke University Divinity School. As an HIV-positive hemophiliac, he has spoken nationwide about AIDS awareness, including on CNN, *Good Morning America*, and Fox News. He and his wife, Pokey, have three daughters and live near Memphis.

Dr. Ronnie Kent recently retired after a forty-one-year practice as a medical doctor in Hattiesburg, Mississippi. He is a graduate of the University of Mississippi and the UM School of Medicine, has been teaching Bible classes in churches for decades, and is the father of three and grandfather of ten. He and his wife, Anne, have been married for forty-four years.

Dr. Ray Cummings has been pastoring churches for more than thirty years. A graduate of William Carey College and New Orleans Baptist Theological

Seminary, he has a doctorate in ministry with a specialization in church growth and evangelism, and he is the coauthor of The 41 Series devotionals. He and his wife, Amanda, have four children and live in Purvis, Mississippi.

Anthony Thaxton is an Emmy Award-winning filmmaker, television producer, and painter. He directed the acclaimed documentary *Walter Anderson: The Extraordinary Life and Art of the Islander*, directed projects with Morgan Freeman and Dolly Parton, and is the producer of *Palate to Palette* on public television. His photography has been featured on *Good Morning America*, CNN, and *Fox & Friends*, and his vibrant watercolors have been featured in books and on numerous television programs. He and his wife, Amy, live in Raymond, Mississippi.

Keelin MacGregor is a collaborative writer, editor, and avid circus artist based in the Pacific Northwest. Coauthor of Amazon #1 new release *Jane Doe #9: A "Surviving R. Kelly" Victim Speaks Out*, covering abuse victim Lizzette Martinez, her most recent collaborative work is *The Deadly Path: How Operation Fast & Furious and Bad Lawyers Armed Mexican Cartels* with government whistleblower and former ATF agent Pete Forcelli.